Discovering Dark Psychology

Mind Manipulation Trilogy: Exploring the Mysteries and Enigmas of Dark Psychology, Volume 3

Ylich Tarazona

Published by Ylich Eduard Tarazona Gil, 2024.

While every precaution has been taken in the preparation of this book, the publisher assumes no responsibility for errors or omissions, or for damages resulting from the use of the information contained herein.

DISCOVERING DARK PSYCHOLOGY

First edition. July 21, 2024.

Copyright © 2024 Ylich Tarazona.

ISBN: 979-8227692689

Written by Ylich Tarazona.

Table of Contents

Discovering Dark Psychology

An exploration of the hidden depths of the mind and its impact on our actions and relationships.

Echoes in the Shadow: How the darkest corners of the human mind shape our thoughts and emotions.

What secrets lurk in the darkest corners of the human mind? How do these hidden shadows influence our decisions, relationships and perceptions of the world? **"Discovering Dark Psychology"**, invites you to dive into an intriguing journey into the core of human nature, and deep into the subconscious where the deepest truths are waiting to be uncovered.

This book is not just a study; it is a guide to understanding the mysterious mechanisms that guide our most enigmatic behavior. With a mix of psychological theories, real case studies and personal reflections, the author unravels the psychology behind our shadiest actions and what they reveal about ourselves.

In this book in its special edition you will learn to:

- Identify the manifestations of dark psychology in everyday life.

- Understand the roots of behaviors such as manipulation, betrayal and seduction of power.

- Transform obscure knowledge into a tool for personal growth and improving your relationships.

Every page of this book challenges your perceptions, confronts you with uncomfortable questions, and equips you with powerful knowledge to confront the darkness that resides within each of us. You won't just read **"Discovering Dark Psychology"**; you will experience it.

Warning: This book may profoundly alter your understanding of yourself and others. Read with caution.

3rd Special Edition revised, updated and extended.

YLICH TARAZONA

Writer and Lecturer

AUTHOR'S RIGHT

Introduction

"Have you ever wondered what dark impulses lurk behind the most disturbing human actions?"

Welcome to a journey through the most hidden recesses of the human mind, a territory where the shadows speak louder than the lights. **"Discovering Dark Psychology"** is not simply a book; it is a bold and profound exploration of those aspects of our psyche that we often prefer to ignore or disregard.

This book is born out of a fascination with the shadow side of human nature: *what drives us to act wickedly? How can seemingly ordinary individuals perform acts of extreme cruelty?* And, most importantly, *what can we learn about ourselves by exploring these dark corners of our existence?*

The objective of **"Discovering Dark Psychology"** is twofold. First, it aims to demystify and clarify the concept of dark psychology, a field that is often misunderstood and shrouded in prejudice. Second, it seeks to provide you with the tools to recognize and confront the manifestations of darkness in your environment and within yourself. In doing so, you will not only increase your self-awareness, but also improve your relationships and make more conscious and ethical decisions in your daily life.

This book is designed to resonate with those who seek to better understand both the world around them and their own inner reactions and emotions. Through case studies, psychological theories, and real-life examples, we will explore how dark psychology manifests itself in everyday life, from the workplace to our most intimate relationships.

As you read these pages, I invite you to keep an open mind and be prepared to face some uncomfortable truths about human nature. This is not a book for the faint of heart, but for those brave enough to look beneath the surface and face what lies there. By the end of this journey, you will not only better understand the dark aspects of human behavior, but you will also be equipped to handle them with wisdom and compassion.

Are you ready to discover what lies in the shadows? Join me on this introspective and revealing journey.

Author's Preface

For as long as I can remember, I have been fascinated by the complexities of the human mind. *What makes us act the way we do? What unseen forces shape our daily decisions, our relationships, and our understanding of right and wrong?* This curiosity led me to study psychology, and ultimately, to write this book, **"Discovering Dark Psychology."**

This work is the result of years of research, study and observation, both in clinical settings and in everyday life. It has been both a professional and deeply personal journey, in which I have explored not only the existing literature, but also my own perceptions and experiences of human nature.

Dark psychology, often viewed with caution and even fear, actually offers an invaluable window into the full understanding of human behavior. This book aims to unveil those aspects of our psyche that we prefer to ignore: the dark corners where manipulation, deception and, at times, cruelty brew. My intention is not to glorify these tendencies, but to understand them in order to better confront and prevent them.

In these pages, I share with you theories and case studies that illustrate how darkness manifests itself in everyday life. Beyond the descriptions and analyses, however, I have included reflections and practical tools to help readers identify and combat negative influences in their own lives and environment.

Writing this book has not been an easy task. It has required revisiting personal beliefs and confronting uncomfortable truths about what we human beings are capable of. But I believe that, ultimately, the self-knowledge that dark psychology provides is a crucial step toward greater understanding and empathy for one another.

I thank everyone who has been part of this journey, from colleagues and mentors to family and friends who have supported and guided me along the way. And to you, reader, I especially thank you for opening this book and joining me on this exploration of the obscure, but fascinating, nature of the human mind.

Dedication

To you, intrepid explorer of the mysteries of the human mind,

This book is for you, who have chosen to embark on a journey into the hidden depths of human psychology. With courage and an open mind, you enter the labyrinths of our darkest inclinations, seeking to understand the incomprehensible and face what many choose to ignore.

I dedicate these pages to your tireless quest for knowledge, your commitment to self-understanding and your audacity to look beyond the apparent. This book is a tribute to your curiosity and courage, tools with which you will unravel the innermost secrets of human nature.

I hope this journey transforms, challenges and inspires you. May you find in each chapter a mirror of your own experiences and a map to a deeper understanding of those around you. May this exploration equip you with a new perspective on human behavior, strengthening your empathy and your ability to act with wisdom and compassion.

Thank you for not only being a reader, but a companion on this journey toward discovering the shadows that shape our lives. Together, we will illuminate those dark corners with the glow of understanding and hope.

With deep respect and appreciation for your courage, YLICH TARAZONA.

Section

"In each of us there is a hidden side, a dark ocean of secrets that we barely understand. Plunging into that abyss is the first step toward true self-understanding."

- Anonymous.

This epigraph captures the essence of "**Discovering Dark Psychology**," inviting you to venture into the uncharted territories of your own mind. Here, "*darkness*" does not simply symbolize evil or the negative, but all that is hidden beneath the surface: *the fears, desires, and motivations that we rarely see in full light.* Diving into this *'dark ocean'* is challenging, it can be intimidating, but it is essential to reach a full and compassionate understanding of ourselves and others.

Each chapter of this book guides you deeper into that understanding, using darkness not as a place of fear, but as a space of revelation. In exploring these depths, we not only discover what binds us to others, but also learn how our shadows can, ironically, illuminate our path to personal growth and empathy. This epigraph, then, not only introduces the themes of the book, but also challenges and encourages each reader to courageously face those aspects of themselves that are rarely examined.

CHAPTER I: FUNDAMENTAL FACTS ABOUT DARK PSYCHOLOGY

What Is Dark Psychology?

"You can't see it, you can't feel it, you can't hear it, you can't smell it. It hides behind the stars and under the hills and fills the empty holes. It comes first and follows after. It ends life, it kills laughter."

- J.R.R Tolkien, "The Hobbit".

The mind is one of the most complex aspects of human nature. Its workings have puzzled and intrigued mankind since time immemorial. Philosophers, psychologists and scientists have tried to unravel its mysteries. There is a general belief that the human mind influences our behavior and actions. Therefore, much effort has been devoted to understanding the mental process a person goes through before acting, either positively or negatively.

Brain Studies

Some attempts to study the human mind have focused on the brain. These studies examine the physical aspects of the brain, focusing on how information is acquired, processed, interpreted and stored. Essentially, they seek to better understand how the brain can affect a person's way of reasoning. These studies have led to advances in the management of debilitating conditions such as Alzheimer's disease, perceptual difficulties and even memory loss.

Psychology and Emotions

The most familiar aspect of the study of the human mind is psychology. At some point in our lives, we have consulted a psychologist or known someone who has done so to deal with our most difficult emotional battles. Many times, life experiences bring us down in ways that we cannot repair on our own. Sometimes, the cause of that breakdown is certain biological markers inherited from our parents. Emotions such as depression, anxiety and fear obscure our daily experiences, hindering our development. With a combination of medication and therapy, we can protect ourselves from the darkness within.

The Darkness in Others

We all have the capacity to do great things. We also possess the capacity to do great harm. Beneath emotions such as sadness, depression, joy and happiness, deep desires are hidden that can lead us to deliberately harm others if we do not control them. These dark desires are rooted in more primal instincts, such as the fight or flight response that promotes our survival. Sometimes, there is only one word that qualifies the human response to these dark emotions: evil.

Dark psychology is the study of the human condition as it relates to the psychological nature of humans to prey on others. In simple terms, dark psychology explores that aspect of human nature that allows us to take deliberate and willful actions that harm our fellow humans. It should be noted that the use of "preying" in this context does not necessarily translate into physical harm to a person, although there is a branch of dark psychology devoted to this. In later chapters, we will briefly touch on those areas to better understand the subject.

The Darkness Within

In movies or books, you may have encountered words or phrases that allude to "an inner darkness." Even some of the most famous philosophers made references to this. The Christian holy book talks about how "the heart of man is desperately wicked." We have all met someone we describe as exceptionally quiet or reserved in social settings, only to have this same person commit an act so wicked that we find it difficult to associate that act with that person. Sometimes, it is we ourselves who act this way. Surprising as it may seem, it is not entirely unexpected.

Triggered Responses

These cases are just responses triggered by external situations. The "cauldron" was stirred, so to speak, and those dark emotions that were hidden came to the surface. They usually recede once control is exercised. We all have a latent tendency to be a little naughty or downright mean if the right "buttons" are pushed. Some people, on the other hand, have full control of these dark emotions. They nurture them, feed them and, when it suits them, unleash them at someone else's expense.

Manipulation and Control

Sometimes these emotions are cultivated from an early age. A child learns that if he cries in a certain way, the adults around him will rush to do his bidding. If parents do not teach the child the wrongness of this early on, the child grows up thinking that he can manipulate people to do his will. Crying ceases to be a tool as they grow older, but they continue in their manipulative ways. Where they don't use tears, they use emotions to blackmail their victims. Thus, what began as innocent childish behavior becomes a dark need to control.

Studying Dark Psychology

The intensity of a person's actions defines how far he will go to exert his control. Dark psychology is dedicated to studying the thought process of such a person. It seeks to understand the motive behind these actions, the patterns exhibited before and after carrying them out, and sheds light on how a person can deliberately execute these actions, knowing the pain and harm they could cause another individual. Dark psychology illuminates the dark side of human nature.

The Effects And Impacts Of Dark Psychology

"When you light a candle, you also cast a shadow."
- Ursula K. Le Guin

Introduction

With the little knowledge we now have about dark psychology, we know that some of the most shocking crimes are rooted in certain personality traits related to it. But that's a broader side effect. I want to bring it home to you and I. How does this dark psychology affect us? I assure you there is no "if" in this question, and in a few moments we will understand how.

Effects on Perpetrator and Victim

The effects of dark psychology are experienced by both the perpetrator and the victim. To understand the impacts, we need to explore some elements of dark psychology. People who exhibit certain personality traits considered dark, such as narcissism, psychopathy, and Machiavellianism, tend to experience difficulties in all aspects of their relationships. If a person exhibits all three traits, he or she has an increased propensity to commit crimes. These three personality traits have specific defining characteristics.

Narcissism

Narcissism is characterized by a sense of entitlement, feelings of superiority, deep-seated envy of the success of others, and exploitative behavior.

Psychopathy

Psychopathy is defined by the absence of guilt, lack of empathy, impulsive and destructive behavior, egocentrism and inability to accept responsibility.

Machiavellianism

Machiavellianism manifests itself through manipulative, selfish and ruthless behavior.

Impact on Labor Relations

Separately, these traits are problematic, but together they can cause major problems, especially in a person's relationships with others. In the workplace, for example, that person:

- You will underperform even in the most mundane tasks.

- You will disrupt the flow of work due to your inability to get along with others.

- It will be intensely hated by others.

- Her impulsiveness will lead her to make questionable and unethical decisions.

- If you are in an administrative position, you are more likely to commit white-collar crime.

Impact on Personal Relationships

But it is not only their work relationships that suffer. In their personal relationships, they will face the following problems:

- Their constant need for attention and validation can exhaust their partner, resulting in short-lived relationships.

- They resort to physical and emotional blackmail to manipulate their partners.

- They tend to be verbally, emotionally or physically abusive to their partners or children.

- People who interact with them pay a high emotional cost.

Personal and Social Consequences

If you have met a person whose relationships are characterized by these experiences, for your mental and emotional well-being, stay away from them. If, on the other hand, you are the one experiencing this, seek the psychological help you need to get better. No matter how deep-seated these problems are, you can improve your behavior and experiences with the right therapy. The first step is to recognize the situation for what it is, admit you have a problem, and seek help immediately.

For the rest of us, dealing with people who have the above traits leaves us emotionally and mentally drained. Sometimes the effect can be physical and, in extreme cases, fatal. The sweet neighbor whose ordeal led me to write this book lost everything physically: her home, her business, her finances. But her loss was much deeper and more significant. We did not have a relationship with the perpetrator of the act, but we became victims as well. Our losses were not as monumental as his, but we experienced losses as well. For starters, we lost our sweet neighbor. She didn't die, but she never recovered from the experience. We lost our ability to trust strangers. Even our relationships with each other seemed to require an additional layer of trust to thrive.

Sense of Loss and Cycle of Abuse

The greatest impact of dark psychology on anyone is that it produces a strong sense of loss. We lose our valuables, our relationships, we lose ourselves and, for those extremely unfortunate, we lose our lives. All things considered, it is safe to say that the impact of this darkness is profound.

Dark Traits and Crime Rates

According to experts, if a person exhibits one of the dark personality traits, there is a strong tendency for him or her to exhibit the others as well. In society in general, if the majority of its members exhibit these traits, it is safe to say that crime rates in that society would be significantly high. This does not mean that people who live in cities or countries with more crime are more likely to be criminals. There are other contributing factors to consider. But the possibility cannot be ruled out entirely.

Domino Effect and the Value of the Intervention

What cannot be ruled out is the ripple effect of actions directly related to dark personality traits. There are certain destructive behaviors that turn victims into predators, and this cycle continues until someone has the courage to break it. Children from abusive homes, for example, often grow up to be abusers. In some cases, in their attempt to break out of the parental mold, they find themselves trapped in equally abusive relationships, even if they are not the abusers. It is almost as if they have a gravitational pull toward the violent elements that characterized their childhood home.

For others, becoming a victim can have such a tremendous impact on their psyche that it causes an internal "break". I have read that this "breakdown" can be temporary. In a brief moment, they lose all control over their primitive instincts and act purely based on the strongest emotion that arises, which is usually anger. It is this condition that leads some people to claim temporary insanity. But there are those who embrace the dark emotions that emerge when they "snap." All sense of morality disappears. The consequences of this are often devastating.

Everyday Examples Of Different Aspects Of Dark Psychology

Dark Behavior in Everyday Life

When you think of dark behaviors, it's understandable that you might think they only apply to crimes that get you on the front page of the newspapers or become long-running movies on the crime channel. In reality, it also includes many things that have become socially acceptable, even if we don't personally condone such behavior. We witness these actions in our homes, schools, offices and, thanks to innovative technology, we now also see them on the Internet. To help you get a clearer picture and hopefully a deeper understanding of this topic, I will share with you some of the more sensational crimes and seemingly insignificant actions that led to a terrible end.

Case Study One

News: Brutal murder of a 14-year-old boy.

Perpetrator Traits: Controlling, abusive, manipulative, reclusive.

Channel: Online games.

This is the tragic story of a young man from a well-structured family. He had the same privileges as any teenager of his age and social group. He had an understanding mother and a father who went out of his way to provide. His mother took every precaution to protect her son from the invasive world of the Internet. Playing online games was just another common activity among teenagers. As long as he didn't spend more than adequate time at it, he should be fine.

However, the perpetrator, only four years older, had sinister plans. Carefully manipulating his young and impressionable victim with lies, he tricked the boy into visiting him at his home, where he committed the heinous crime. It was one of the most disturbing cases, especially considering the age of the victim and the perpetrator. However, regardless of his age, the perpetrator displayed all the predatory traits linked to dark psychology and ended a life just to assert his control.

Case Study Two

News: Worst case of domestic violence.

Perpetrator Traits: Physically abusive, manipulative, controlling.

Channel: Relationship.

Love is a beautiful thing. When you enter into a relationship, you do so with the hope that this person will love and care for you. That you will nurture and protect each other. In the modern parlance of love, it's you and the person against the world. And so this relationship began. A single mother working hard to care for and provide for her son met a charming man who was basically what she had always dreamed of in a partner.

He was charming, considerate and seemed to love his son as much as he loved her. In order to be completely available to this young family, he quit his job and devoted himself to caring for her, until his true dark nature emerged. Using his love for her family, he manipulated her into isolating herself from those who loved her most. He orchestrated the loss of her job, which resulted in the loss of her home. This ensured that she was completely dependent on him. He moved her into his apartment where she was constantly subjected to inhumane torture 24 hours a day.

The careful manipulation of the woman was so effective that, when given the choice of how she preferred to be killed, she actually considered the idea because she felt she had no choice and deserved no better. Chance and an act of bravery on her part led to her rescue and the imprisonment of the perpetrator.

Case Study Three

News: Prominent minister of God accused of abusing minors.

Perpetrator traits: Manipulative, controlling, self-centered.

Channel: Religion.

There is a sacred relationship between religious leaders and their followers. The leader must be the moral compass that guides the followers on the right path. For years, regardless of religion, leaders have abused their position of power, choosing to play the biblical role of the proverbial wolf in sheep's clothing. Instead of being shepherds, they choose to be wolves.

Having established his authenticity by claiming to have direct communication with God, this religious leader deceived his followers with his vision. At one point, he proclaimed himself to be God and claimed to have the mandate to sleep with seven virgins who were also minors. He was subsequently brought to trial and convicted of the crime.

Lessons and Reflections

These three cases are sensational, but the lesson is what I want to draw your attention to. These crimes were not random or spontaneous. They involved careful orchestration that groomed the victims and lulled them into a false state of confidence and security before striking. In fact, the way the events unfolded is reminiscent of the game between a predator and its prey. First, the victim is stalked and observed. Then, based on the information obtained during the observation process, the predator makes its move. Only this move is not to attack, but to charm its prey. To make it feel loved and cared for. It is as if they are wearing a mask and displaying characteristics that they know will attract their victims.

Gradually, trust is established. The next objective is to make the prey dependent on them, whether financially, emotionally or spiritually. The result is the same: they want to feel needed. Then, they isolate their prey, after which, they strike. It's never like those crimes you suspect or see coming from afar. It's like a song and dance routine that gives the predator an advantage and leaves the victim vulnerable.

In the next chapter, we will discuss how vulnerable we are.

How Vulnerable Are We To Dark Psychology?

Examining Our Vulnerability

In examining the case studies used to illustrate the effects of dark psychology in our daily lives, the question of our vulnerability comes to light. The channels these perpetrators used are somewhat innocent and not exactly what one would classify as a precursor to disaster. Therefore, it is safe to say that it is the basis on which these platforms were used that led to the terrible outcome. In the first case, you have a kid in a gaming chat room for his peers. His passion for gaming led him there, but it was his need to connect with friends that informed his decisions and it was this need that the predator took advantage of.

Case Studies and Vulnerability

In the second case study, again, it was a basic human need to connect with someone on an intimate level that was exploited, and the victim's emotions were manipulated to alter her reality. From love, she descended into an emotional state of worthlessness and the perpetrator inflicted more harm because of her vulnerable state. And in the third case, the victims placed their faith in the wrong deity, although his intentions were correct and very human. The predator presented himself as a vital link to what they desired to achieve spiritually, and this desire became the basis of their undoing.

Other cases I have studied follow this same pattern. The emotional wants and needs of the victims were twisted and used against them. This gives credence to the belief that our needs and desires are what make us vulnerable to these predators. Does this mean we should shut down our emotions? Let's reflect on this.

Our Humanity as a Source of Vulnerability and Strength

We have been taught to show strength, not to give in and to never let anyone see our fears. That's because we have been taught that going against these instructions would result in people seeing you as weak and vulnerable. Ironically, what separates us from other creatures is also the source of our strength and weakness: our humanity. We are vulnerable simply because we are human. Our desires, our hopes, our aspirations, our quest for a transcendent life are some of the things that make us vulnerable.

But the day we cease to possess any of these things, we cease to be human, and when we cease to be human, we become the very thing we are trying to protect ourselves from. When we stop believing, when we stop caring or when we stop being vulnerable, we become those seemingly soulless individuals whose only mission is to satisfy their desires with brutality, no matter who they harm in the process. That said, while we recognize that our humanity makes us vulnerable, we must not forget that we can also draw strength from it.

The Need for Human Connection

This brings me to the biologically ingrained human need to connect with others. Let's recognize that this need is a healthy human emotional need. Without connection to another human being, we do not function properly. In fact, I read about a study where test subjects were isolated and studied. Short periods of isolation increased anxiety levels and affected productivity. Long periods of isolation had even worse side effects. Subjects became depressed and began to have dark thoughts for long periods of time.

Consequences of Isolation

Her mental health was not the only thing that suffered. Physically, their sleeping and eating patterns changed. They lost track of time and gradually lost touch with reality. They began to experience early paranoia. The conclusion was that we need contact with other humans to thrive. This need to connect with others makes us vulnerable because people have different agendas for making connections. Some genuinely seek to build good relationships, others just want to use people to gain some other goal such as wealth or influence. For others, their intentions are even more sinister. The secret to navigating this maze of human agendas is knowledge.

The Value of Knowledge

There was a time when the saying "ignorance is bliss" was promoted in many circles as a mantra to emphasize the burden of responsibility that comes with knowledge. I assure you that the price of ignorance is far greater than the burden that knowledge brings. And if you want to win this mental war against the tempting influences of dark psychology, you need wisdom and the right application of knowledge in what you do. Giving up feelings may seem like the ideal solution, but there are recorded cases where this resulted in even greater losses. Choosing to be distrustful and becoming a recluse made victims even more vulnerable and susceptible to a predatory attack.

The Importance of Remaining Open and Cautious

So, instead of closing off opportunities to build relationships with others, you should keep yourself open, but be cautious about your needs and feelings. I am also aware of cases where the victim's emotional needs overpowered their rational thinking. And this is what put them in danger. Our emotions can act as a navigation system that guides you to your needs and there are certain emotions that act as your biological defenses against threats like the ones we've been talking about. And as we explore the topic in detail, you will understand what those emotions are; as well as how to train yourself to recognize those emotions. Until then, if you take anything away from this chapter, it should be the knowledge that yes, you are vulnerable. But, by recognizing and accepting those vulnerabilities, you can turn your greatest weaknesses into your greatest strengths.

CHAPTER II: ANALYZING DARK PSYCHOLOGY

Manipulation, Persuasion Or Influence

"Manipulation fueled with good intentions can be a blessing. But when used maliciously, it is the beginning of a magician's karmic calamity."
- T. F. Hodge.

Manipulation in Simple Terms

In simple terms, to manipulate someone is to control or influence that person in a cunning or unscrupulous manner. Whether we like it or not, we have all manipulated a person or a situation to obtain a desirable outcome. It sounds dark, but let me lighten the mood with a story from my naughty childhood.

A Childhood Story

When I was a child, I had a habit of conveniently getting sick when I didn't want to go to school. Initially, my parents indulged me whenever this happened. After two emergency visits to the clinic, my mother became suspicious of my trickery. The next few times, they did not take me to the clinic, but allowed me to stay home. During one of my stomach pain episodes, my friends called me excitedly to inform me that a local actor would be visiting the school. I ran to my mother begging her to take me back to school, forgetting that I had "unbearable stomach pain." My mother told me she wasn't going to take any chances and that I should stay home. No amount of pleading could change her mind, even after admitting that I had faked the pain. When I arrived at school the next day, I was green with envy as my friends showed me all the cool stuff the actor had brought them. Suffice it to say, I never again faked being sick to stay home from school.

Everyday Manipulation

This story is just one of many when it comes to the things we do to manipulate a situation. I still know many adults who fake a cold to get a day off work.

That's not all bad, is it? Sometimes, we have been manipulated into making decisions that are beneficial to us. A friend gives you a good pair of running shoes and a month's subscription to a local gym; you know he wants you to improve your fitness. Have you ever gone on a lunch date with a friend only to find a potential date and a sudden emergency (of course, from your friend)? I've been there. Interestingly, when we feel threatened, one of the techniques we employ to get out of that unpleasant situation, if brute force is not an option, is also manipulation.

Manipulation as Part of Our Nature

That is to say, the art of manipulation is part of our nature. However, when it comes to psychological manipulation, things get darker and more sinister. In this situation, a person's actions or thoughts are influenced through the use of dishonest tactics that are abusive, deceptive or both. In this context, the person being manipulated has no choice to accept or reject the will of the manipulator. They are simply coerced into compliance.

Manipulators' Motives

Manipulators have their reasons for doing what they do. Sometimes, it's something as basic as financial gain, like the fictitious soldier who tricked my neighbor out of her life savings. In the workplace, these people are committed to promoting their own personal agenda, even if it means pitting one against the other. Their principle is very simple: if you want it, you have to reach out and take it. In relationships, it's often about gaining power and maintaining control. The need to be in charge fuels everything they do, and sometimes they can go to extremes to achieve it. And then there are those who love to manipulate people for recreational reasons. They are simply bored and use their manipulative games to pass the time. It's crude and vicious, but that's how they think.

Common Manipulator Tactics

One of the most common tactics employed by manipulators is lying. A master manipulator is skilled in the art of deception. They are adept at concocting tall tales that have no real basis in truth. Or they resort to subterfuge and lie by omission. Some people are so good at their lies that you almost never notice the lie until it is too late. Another tactic employed by manipulators is guilt-tripping and shaming. When confronted about something they have done wrong, they immediately deny it and then turn the tables by making you feel bad for questioning them in the first place. To strengthen their control over their victim, they vilify them, effectively turning the victim into the abuser. You will find this type of manipulative technique in domestic cases, where the abuser will claim that the victim's character, words or actions are what provoked their behavior in the first place.

Other Subtle Techniques

Other subtle techniques used in manipulation include the use of evasive and noncommittal answers to questions asked. Rationalizing their actions if caught and spinning reality to match their narrative. Some manipulators employ sex and seduction to accomplish their perverse goals. When caught red-handed, anger and projection of guilt are quickly used to manipulate the situation in their favor.

Dam Selection

However, manipulators are not always random in their selection of prey. There are certain traits in their victims that attract them, and certain vulnerabilities also make it easier for the manipulator to perpetuate their crimes. Lonely people with low self-esteem and a desire to please are easier to control than the assertive social type. Although, there are people who exhibit characteristics similar to the latter group who also end up being manipulated. For these people, manipulators study their personality flaws and weaknesses before using them against them. Impressionable people are prone to be fooled by appearances. Abrupt individuals who tend to make compulsive decisions are more likely to be manipulated into making hasty decisions that have a long-term impact. Greedy and materialistic people have a greater tendency to be conned.

Deception - The Truth Behind The Lie

"Just because something is not a lie, does not mean it is not deceptive. A liar knows he is a liar. But he who tells mere portions of truth to deceive is a craftsman of destruction."
- Criss Jami.

Definition of Deception

Deception is defined as the act of concealing the truth, especially to gain an advantage. This may look like manipulation, but there is a distinct difference. Deception is often employed in the act of manipulation and is one of many layers in the scheme of a manipulator. The goal of deception is to mislead and confuse the other party. While manipulation is much more profound, this does not negate the adverse effects of deception. A lie may take a long time to be discovered, but when it is discovered, the damage and destruction it leaves in its wake can be devastating.

Story of a Marriage

I know the story of a man who was married for over 25 years. That marriage produced three children between the ages of 11 and 17. Everything was going well for the family. The children attended the best schools and enjoyed the luxuries of life thanks to the wealth gained through years of hard work and resilience on the man's part. He pampered his children by making sure to provide them with everything they needed. And who could blame him? For the first seven years of their marriage, the couple was unable to conceive. They sought the help of specialists, spiritualists and even tried some unorthodox practices, all to no avail. At a low point in their marriage, his wife became pregnant. He was elated. When the couple had two more children, it seemed like things couldn't get any better, but they did. Their wealth grew exponentially and the timing was perfect.

One day, the couple received a call that their oldest son had been in an accident. A life-saving operation involving organ donation was required. In the process of donating his organ to save his son, he discovered the terrible secret his wife had kept for many years. The child was not his. In fact, none of the children were. Shattered, hurt and ashamed, he took his own life, but not before cutting his wife and children off from his wealth. This deception began as a lie to one person, but at the end of the day, five people (including the deceiver) were affected by it. Not to mention the pain experienced by extended family, friends and colleagues.

History of a Company

In another situation, a young company enlisted the services of an accountant to handle its financial affairs. The owner of the start-up quickly took a liking to this young accountant. It was strictly a business relationship, but there was also a sense of friendship. As the company grew and expanded its operations, the business owner delegated most of the administrative responsibilities to the accountant. He proved to be competent and was entrusted with even more responsibilities. These responsibilities came with many benefits and, for a while, things were going well. But when a failed transaction prompted a quick review of the company's records, the owner was unprepared for the revelation that unfolded. For years, he and his company had been systematically ripped off to the point where the company's accounts were in the red. The accountant fled and he was left to clean up the mess. Within months, the company closed. 43 people lost their jobs, the business owner lost his entire investment and his ability to trust.

The Crude Nature of Deception

The crux of deception is that it is based on the emotion essential to the human relationship: trust. For an act of deception to work, a form of relationship must be established between the deceiver and the victim. The greater the trust, the greater the betrayal. And when there is deep betrayal, the destructive impact often goes beyond the two individuals involved.

Self-Deception

However, deception is not always something we do to others. Sometimes, it is the lies we tell ourselves. We justify certain actions with the deep lies we tell ourselves. Like manipulation, lying is something we all do. Some of us may have developed certain moral principles that make it difficult for us to tell blatant lies or associate with people who do. But that doesn't stop us from telling lies, even if they are "little" lies. Knowing the answer to a question, but choosing to deny knowledge of it to preserve social grace is a lie.

Example of an Everyday Situation

Let me explain, let's say you witnessed your boss throwing a colleague's project [something they worked very hard on] in the trash and listened as he talked at length about how horrible he thinks the idea is. You fumble and then leave the office only to be confronted by said colleague asking about the boss's opinions on the project. Telling the truth in this case would do more harm than good. And so, you lie. Your intention to mislead your colleague was for his own good.

Deception in Dark Psychology

In dark psychology, the intention to deceive presents more benefits to the deceiver than to the victim. As mentioned earlier, manipulators use deception to strengthen their control over their victims. For deceivers, deception gives them an opportunity to develop a relationship with the victim. The goal is to exploit this relationship for their benefits. One of the most recent forms of deception employed today is deceptive affection. People who claim to feel more love or emotion for you than they really do.

Deceptive Affection

Not many things can describe the feeling of someone telling you that they love you. This is especially gratifying for people who have longed for this experience. The deceiver reaps the benefits of declaring this false affection in the form of trust, sex, and sometimes money.

Hypnosis - The Power Of Hypnotic Suggestion

"The scientific dictator of tomorrow will install his whispering machines and subliminal projectors in schools and hospitals (children and the sick are highly suggestible) and in all public places where audiences can undergo a preliminary preparation of suggestibility - increasing oratory or rituals."
- Aldous Huxley.

First Encounter with Hypnosis

Some time ago, the idea of hypnosis was relegated to the world of fantasy. That a person's mind could be controlled by the swinging of an object and the snapping of fingers was considered unbelievable. My first encounter with hypnosis was at a magic show. The magician called an audience member on stage and then put her "under." In that state, she did some strange things that I'm pretty sure she would have been mortified to do in her right mind. When the magician brought her out of that state, she had no idea what had happened in the last two minutes. Admittedly, someone could have that much power over you and make you do things you wouldn't normally do is terrifying. So I understand why we have chosen to deny it.

The Reality of Hypnosis

However, no amount of denial can change the fact that hypnosis is real and is used far more often than we are willing to admit. In modern psychology today, hypnotherapy has been effective in the treatment of certain skin conditions and is also used in the management of pain associated with childbirth, dental procedures and even rheumatoid arthritis. While hypnosis is certainly not the typical "pat on the cheek and do as I say," certain people are more susceptible to hypnosis than others. But let's not get ahead of ourselves.

Definition of Hypnosis

Hypnosis in psychology is described as a cooperative interaction in which participants respond to the suggestions of the hypnotist. That is, when a person is hypnotized, his or her actions are strongly guided by the hypnotist. In movies, we are led to believe that a person under hypnosis becomes drowsy and disoriented. In reality, people react differently under hypnosis, but they are not as incapacitated as they appear to be. In fact, psychologists refer to this as a state of hyper-awareness. In this state, they experience focused attention, heightened suggestibility and vivid fantasies. People are brought into this state through the use of visualization and verbal repetition.

Who Can Be Hypnotized

This tells us that not everyone can hypnotize [clearly, you need to possess a keen ability to visualize things]. One article I read put the percentage of people [adults] who cannot hypnotize themselves at 10%. That leaves about 90% of us susceptible, which is shocking considering how strongly many of us feel about hypnotism. I suspect that some of the negative feelings we have about hypnotism are due to misguided beliefs about it. Here are some of the most common misconceptions:

1. Hypnotism puts you under the total control of your hypnotist.

In the movies, we are led to believe that a person under hypnosis would have their actions controlled by the hypnotist. In reality, this is not true. While hypnosis is largely based on suggestions, if your mind does not agree with those suggestions, you would reject them immediately. So no, you won't be crawling on all fours and mooing like a cow... unless you want to.

2. You might not be able to come out of hypnosis.

The mind is more complex than we think. The same self-protection mechanisms that make it almost impossible for your hypnotist to control your actions also keep you alert and, if there is any immediate danger, you can come out of hypnosis in an instant.

3. Hypnosis is some kind of dark magic or spiritual event.

Sorry to disappoint you, but this is pure science. It is based on the research work of renowned psychologists such as Sigmund Freud. There is a method and a process to it, and none of it requires wooden dummies and red candles. All that is needed is your consent.

4. You can hypnotize yourself against your will.

Again, we have Hollywood to thank for this kind of thinking. A man gets on stage and hypnotizes an entire crowd to do his bidding? Given what we now know, not likely. Like I said, they need your consent.

5. Hypnosis can improve your skills.

This is both true and false. It depends on what you are looking at. Hypnosis can improve your memory, but it can also give you false memories or distort that same memory. So, the results aren't as great as you'd expect. It has also been linked to improved performance, but don't expect to be running a 5k marathon overnight.

Hypnosis in the Hands of People with Dark Intentions

Now that we have looked objectively at hypnosis and what it is, I can tell you that, in the hands of a psychopath or a person with dark intentions, hypnosis can also be dangerous. Hypnosis does not always involve you going into a trance state for it to be effective. The key elements in hypnosis are the power of suggestion and the repetitive use of words that resonate deeply with the victim. Politicians, for example, exploit this in their campaigns. They use words like change, make a difference, etc. These words trigger a deeper search within oneself and, subconsciously, we find ourselves desiring that change.

Hypnosis in Personal Relationships

There are situations where it seems that one person is completely fascinated by another. A few suggestive words from this person and the victim runs to do their bidding. In books, articles and even in real life situations, you may hear or read the description of a particular relationship as "being under a spell". This is the power of hypnosis. This hypnosis does not refer to that performed on the psychologist's couch. It is more intimate, and the resulting effect can be just as devastating. Parents have abandoned their children, handing over all their wealth to a complete stranger because of this.

Problem Behavior

"Technological progress is like an axe in the hands of a pathological criminal."
- Albert Einstein.

Introduction

The topic of criminal behavior is not the primary focus of this book, but it cannot be overlooked, as it constitutes an aspect of obscure psychology. Profilers, criminologists, and law enforcement agencies benefit greatly from the study of criminal behavior. In psychology, the term criminal behavior is not often used because there is a general consensus that crime is a behavior, and engaging in a crime does not necessarily make someone a criminal. Of course, there is much debate about this type of thinking, but we should leave that to the experts. Here we will focus on the elements that make a person commit a crime.

Exploring the Use of Dark Psychology to Do Harm

Specifically, I want us to explore why people employ the use of dark psychology to harm others. This harm can be physical or emotional. But before we delve into this, I must draw your attention to something important. Certain people do things simply because they can. Not because they were driven by some childhood pain or a need to get revenge for an offense you may not even have committed. They do it simply because they can.

As humans, it is our nature to try to understand why. We want to make sense of our situation rather than believing that we are simply victims of random acts. But we must also be prepared to accept that sometimes, the situation really is as it seems: a person driven by his or her own personal desire to harm others. If you bought this book looking for answers to questions like that, you must also be open to the possibility that this person is simply evil.

Characteristics of Offensive Behavior

For a person to commit a certain type of offense, he or she generally displays certain characteristics that indicate that this person may be capable of it. This goes beyond judging a book by its cover because prolific criminals are often masters of disguise. They charm you right before they disarm you. In our daily lives, these people disguise themselves as one of us, pretending to have your best interests at heart. Given what we now know about manipulation, deception and hypnosis, we are aware that predators are not always strangers.

How to Detect Problem Behavior

So how can you detect those things that help you make better decisions when relating to people? For this chapter, I'm going to address four traits. As we go deeper, we will explore these traits and more in detail.

1. Family and Friends

You know that saying: tell me who you hang out with and I'll tell you who you are? Besides yourself, examine the circles in which this person moves. Do they come from a close-knit family? How is their relationship with their family? Have you met their friends? If this person has no friends at all, it could be a red flag.

2. History

We like the idea of a person being completely reformed and, in all honesty, this does happen. However, you should not ignore the fact that a person with a negative history has a greater tendency to become a repeat offender. If the person was abusive in their previous relationship, there is a chance they will be the same with you. Unless they have been in treatment or are actively receiving treatment.

3. Control Problems

People who lack the ability to control themselves in situations that provoke them have a propensity to hurt others. Likewise, people who have a problem giving up control have it in them to snap and lash out at the nearest victim when they lose control, and that person could be you.

4. Antisocial Values

In social settings, watch your interactions with others. People who are generally unpleasant to everyone are red flags. They don't have to be pleasant to everyone, but if the person is generally obnoxious, rude and has trouble getting along with people, you could have a problem on your hands.

5. Substance Abuse

Dependence on any type of drug or alcohol is a clear indicator that this person is dealing with certain problems. Substance abuse negates your ability to reason properly and make sound decisions. A person who abuses drugs or alcohol may not be in a position to treat your relationship as a priority in their life. And unless they have a way to sustain that lifestyle, you could end up paying for it directly or indirectly. This can lead to years of abuse and neglect.

Guidelines for Identifying Criminal Behavior

These are only indications of criminal elements in the people we relate to. As with all things human, there are exceptions and variables. But the biggest mistake you can make is to see clear indications and then simply rationalize them away. We have a tendency to make excuses for others. The first thing we tell ourselves is that no one is perfect. But that ideology can quickly get us into trouble. Get informed, stay aware and make informed decisions. This doesn't guarantee that you can stop these guys from hurting you and taking advantage of you. But you can protect yourself from them 100% better than if you act from a place of ignorance.

The Danger of Wanting to Fix Others

Some of us are inherently programmed to want to fix the people in our lives. We see someone who is obviously broken and think that, if we love them enough, we can bring them back from the edge of whatever cliff they are on and begin our journey to a happily ever after. From my personal experiences, as well as the shared experience of others, I can tell you with confidence that this is highly unlikely to work. The best case scenario is that you break down and spend a better part of your life healing from something you could have easily walked away from before.

Reverse Psychology

"Sometimes, I push you away...because I secretly hope you'll draw me closer."
- Anonymous.

Definition and Use of Reverse Psychology

Reverse psychology is a more refined form of manipulation. Technically, it is defined as a technique that involves the assertion of a belief or behavior that is opposite to that which is desired, with the expectation that this approach will encourage the subject of persuasion to do what is actually desired. The main difference between reverse psychology and manipulation is that the person being manipulated is given the illusion of choice. He is made to believe that he is making a decision to do what he wants, but in reality, he has been subtly coerced into doing exactly what the manipulator wants. Pretty ingenious when you think about the mental process involved in carrying this out, until you find yourself in the same shoes as the victim.

Reverse Psychology in Parenting

Reverse psychology is a technique often used by parents in parenting their children. It works well with children who are considered "resistant" to authority. At first glance, this seems innocent and without obvious harm to the child or their psyche, but it is also known that it can have the opposite effect. In our daily activities, we use reverse psychology in our relationships with others and it is not always born of malicious intent. Let me give an example using a wedding planner and his client.

Example of a Wedding Planner

Let's say this client is very decided about the colors they want to wear on their wedding day. Nothing wrong with that, except that the colors in question turn out to be completely gaudy and outlandish, especially in comparison to the exotic location for the wedding and the prestigious guests that have been invited. Obviously, the wedding planner cannot tell the client that their color choices are too tacky. Instead, what he does is agree with the client and then politely tell a story that hints that a very important guest (who has also been invited to this wedding) criticized a previous event because of a similar color, but quickly adds that he is sure they can pull it off somehow. This causes the client to reflect. He rethinks his choices, the planner gets what he wanted all along.

Reverse Psychology in Marketing

Salespeople use this technique to sell their products to consumers. They agree with their consumer market on certain decisions and, by acknowledging their agreement, they succeed in convincing their customers to buy their services. But it's not just parents and business owners who are guilty of using reverse psychology. We use this technique in dating as well. Most relationship experts will tell you that we are conditioned to want what we can't have. So, in order to make a person like you more or want you more, you make yourself inaccessible to them. It's really a paradox. As with all forms of reverse psychology, it can also fail. Playing hard to get may appeal to a man's hunting instincts, but unless you plan to be elusive forever, you'll have to stop "running." When you stop, the hunter backs off and then you have a stalemate.

Conclusion

Reverse psychology can be a powerful and effective tool, but it can also have unintended consequences if not used carefully. In the right hands and with the right intentions, it can be a way to guide someone toward a decision that is beneficial to both of you. However, when used with bad intentions or without considering the welfare of the other person, it can become detrimental. It is essential to be aware of ethical and emotional boundaries when employing reverse psychology techniques, ensuring that they are used respectfully and with consideration for the feelings and wishes of others.

CHAPTER III: KEY AREAS IN OUR LIVES THAT MAKE US VULNERABLE TO DARK PSYCHOLOGY

Love & Relationships

"Those who seek love only manifest their own lovelessness. And the loveless never find love. Only the loving find love. And they never have to look for it."
- D. H. Lawrence.

Bringing Dark Psychology Closer to Home

Now that we've tackled the creepier side of dark psychology, let's bring things closer to home. Because, let's be honest. You've read all that and probably thought, "This doesn't apply to me; I could never be in that situation." Admittedly, the odds of things getting that horrible are pretty low. But never make the mistake of assuming you are immune to the powers of dark psychology. Its influence is much closer to you than you think. The most common place where elements of dark psychology manifest is in our love relationships with our partner.

The Universal Nature of Love

Love is a universal language. It is a primal emotion that we all instinctively crave. As humans, we are designed to love. We want to love and feel loved. No one is as happy as a man or woman who is in love and knows that he or she is loved in return. Some people mate for procreation. Some people pair up to avoid social pressure. Some even pair up to promote alliance between powerful families. But, the main reason for relationships, i.e., getting a partner, is love. That said, it is easy for things to degrade to a point where love is used as a bargaining chip to gain more power over another person. And this is where elements of dark psychology come into play.

Manipulation in Love Relationships

You've heard the saying "use what you have to get what you want." In the business world, that kind of thinking comes with the territory. But in relationships, it's called manipulation. Let's explore this example. A woman knows that her partner finds her sexually attractive and irresistible. Perhaps there is something she has wanted from him for a long time, but has failed to elicit his willingness to comply despite the long conversations they have had about it. Suppose what she has always wanted from him is his physical contribution in doing household chores.

Her stubborn stance leads her to devise a way to make her partner compliant. She has to do this without directly telling him something like "vacuum the living room or there will be no sex tonight." While that has been known to happen in certain households, it would probably fail, especially if you are dealing with people who have a natural aversion to taking instructions from others, no matter how well worded. So, instead, she bides her time. When she finds him in the middle of doing a random task, she compliments him. She tells him things like how much she finds him attractive when he's doing [whatever she finds him doing] and then satisfies his sexual desire for her.

The Impact of Dark Psychology on Relationships

The impact of this tactic is even greater if he usually has to "work" to get her so aroused. If she does this constantly, he subconsciously gets the message that doing housework might equate to having good sex later. Over time, she programs herself to do the chores she would have naturally turned down because of the sexual motivation her partner offers her.

This scenario seems harmless. But if you look closely, dark psychology was used here. The man was manipulated into willingly doing things for his partner just for sex. She understood his weakness and used it to her advantage to get what she wanted. The advantage is that, in this case, everyone walks away happy. Because the woman gets the valuable contribution she needs from her partner and the man gets the sex he craves with the woman he desires. But things are not always so mutually beneficial when dark psychology is involved. It can get really dark for the victim. Let's look at this other couple.

Case of Dave and Maya

I will call this new couple Dave and Maya. Dave and Maya have very contrasting personalities. Dave is a homebody and Maya is a vivacious extrovert with lots of friends. At first glance, it would seem that their personality differences complement each other perfectly. This was true until Dave felt the need to exert more control over Maya. But he knows (probably because he's already tried) that he can't use direct force to get what he wants. So, he begins a campaign to bring Maya under his control. He starts by criticizing small details about her, like her choice of clothes, makeup, hair and even makes derogatory comments about her weight, under the guise of love, of course.

This begins to affect her confidence and when she mentions her friends, he uses petty incidents to illustrate and back up his theory about some fictitious enmity between them [things like "they're jealous of you" usually work]. These little seeds of doubt grow and fully blossom, creating a rift that separates Maya from her friends. Friendless and with self-esteem issues thanks to her new low confidence, she is made to feel that Dave is the only person who really cares about her and accepts her as she is. This drives her to want to do everything she can to please Dave, putting her exactly where he wants her to be...under his total control.

Reflections on the Cases

In the two cases I used as illustrations, we see instances where relationships, which are supposed to be about the two people involved, become a channel to satisfy a partner's desires through manipulation and deception. Both relationships began with good intentions and, while the outcome of the first proved to be a satisfying situation for both parties, in the second story, the outcome is the opposite. The similarities here are that all the victims did what they did because of their feelings for their partners. Therefore, this shows that our desire to be loved can leave us vulnerable. It can be manipulated and exploited for the benefit of others.

Blind Faith And Religious Belief

"If we seek solace in the prisons of the distant past, security in human systems, we are told that it will always, always last. Emotions are the sail and blind faith is the mast. Without the breath of true freedom, we get nowhere fast."
- Sting.

Introduction

I will say that blind faith does not only refer to belief in a supreme God or higher deity. Some people choose to believe in science. Regardless of what faith you practice, there is one fact: our faith sometimes creates a blind spot that distorts reality, causing us to make decisions we probably wouldn't make if we were in the right frame of mind. But before we get into the "what", let's look at the "why".

Human Vulnerability

When I talked about vulnerability in a previous chapter, I said that the things that make us human are some of the things that make us vulnerable and susceptible to the machinations of dark psychology. For some people, these influences are more obvious than for others. Our beliefs in deities go back even to the earliest civilizations. Man has always considered his existence as a small fraction in the universal scheme of things, so we believe that there are forces that are larger, more powerful and divine. If you examine things logically, this kind of thinking makes sense because it helps our minds deal with the unexplainable things that happen around us.

The Need for Explanations

You see a beautiful flower and marvel at how something so exquisite and delicate can simply exist... no thought, no pattern, it's just there. We look at the vast expanse of the sky and wonder what lies beyond. Does it go on forever? Or does it fade into an endless end? When you hear the mighty roar of a waterfall or the rumbling sounds of thunder, even with the advances and knowledge we have, we still tremble with fear and awe. Back in the day, your choices were to let the fear drive you crazy or rationalize the situation by attributing it to a sovereign being that is greater than you. Some of the braver ones chose to use science to make their explanations.

Fear of Death and the Afterlife

Following this same line of thinking, when someone we love dies, we are forced to confront our own mortality. Our grief is compounded by questions about life and death - does the journey end here or does it continue in the afterlife? This has been a strong motivating force behind current belief systems. The fear and consideration given to life after this life has led many to make the "right choices" here, so that when death comes, the life we hope will continue afterward will be favorable to us. It is our own way of manipulating the end result, so to speak, because the alternative as it has been portrayed to us is so bleak. Some people take advantage of our fear of the afterlife to manipulate us to get what they want.

Religious Leaders and their Influence

If we hold this theory of the afterlife in such high esteem, you can imagine how we treat people who are considered spokespersons for the deities who control the afterlife. Pastors, imams, rabbis and all forms of religious leaders are held in such high reverence that their words are considered the words of the deity in question. In general, these religious leaders must apply morally sound principles in accordance with their respective offices and act in the best interests of their members. If for no other reason, at least to promote the tenets of the faith they claim to represent. However, this is not always the case as we have come to realize. Many religious leaders abuse their roles and influence by misleading their members into making decisions that only serve their selfish agendas.

Tactics of False Religious Leaders

The common tactic is to use the name of the main deity to twist words taken from the religion's sacred manual to mean new things to corroborate whatever story they are making up to help them successfully manipulate people. Many people have been conned, physically hurt and even driven to commit heinous crimes under this pretext. Another method these false leaders use is to claim to have a spiritual vision or insight into a specific need the victim has. They create an elaborate story that is a mixture of lies intertwined with the truth (usually obtained without the victim or third parties knowing) and the main objective is to extort the victim for money, favors or simply to play with power. Some victims are coerced into parting with more money than they can expect to have. In some cases, impressionable young victims are brainwashed to live in fear in quasi-cult-like situations.

Spiritual and Scientific Fraud

But, scenarios like these don't just end up in religious homes. There are people who are not affiliated with any religion, but like to consider themselves spiritually open. These people encounter fake psychics and mediums who claim to have a strong connection to the underworld. Again, our attachment to people who have died, as well as our concerns about what happens after death, cloud our judgments and leave us open to con artists who want to manipulate the situation in their favor. They use the same trick as false religious leaders, employing deception and lies to manipulate their victims. Victims go for a 10-minute psychic reading of their horoscopes and palms only to be sucked in for years with promises, altered realities and false hopes. This causes them to spend thousands and thousands of dollars in search of the elusive "truth."

Science-Based Manipulations

People who place their hope in science are not immune to manipulation. If you think that, because your faith is anchored in readable, factual science, you cannot be influenced, think again. When there is a crisis, people turn to what they believe. For a believer in science, they naturally turn to science. There are cases where people with debilitating medical conditions seek unconventional medicine in an attempt to survive the illness. Knowing that the best of conventional medicine has failed, they turn to these outsiders who claim to have the solution with their experimental drugs and medical procedures never performed. Unfortunately, these procedures are too risky, too expensive and often uninsured. But the slim chance of life is worth every penny and this is what the fraudsters exploit.

Miraculous Solutions and False Promises

And it is not only in crisis. There are people who present wonderful solutions to a massive problem such as weight loss etc. They claim that their latest diet fad, miracle pill or technology can transform us using scientific theories that have not been tested or verified. Many people buy the promise of this transformation based on information that has been specifically manipulated to extort money from victims. The main difference between religious scammers and these promoters of false science is that, instead of a deity, they use science when they scam their victims. And sadly, most people don't realize until it is too late how badly they are being affected.

Conclusion

When it comes to beliefs, those who use dark psychology prey on your deepest needs and exploit them. They use what you hold sacred to manipulate your thought process. And sometimes, the sacredness of it doesn't really matter. As long as it's important to you, they consider it a gold mine of some kind. And there is no better time to "mine" an individual, so to speak, than when that individual is experiencing a crisis. This is because, in your moment of crisis, you are at your weakest and most susceptible to the influences of others, and people have been known to manipulate things to their own advantage.

Social Conditioning

Society's Influence on Our Lives

In a group discussion when I was in school, I heard an argument where someone vehemently stated that we are a product of our society. I wanted to refute it immediately because I knew many successful people who challenged their society and distinguished themselves by achieving very impressive feats. As I grew older and experienced more of life, I realized that these people were "exceptional." It is an undeniable fact that the society we live in plays a tremendous role in shaping us in more ways than we can imagine. The ugly truth is that the way we think, live and function can be traced back to the influences of our society and these are some of the things that dark psychology exploits.

What is Social Conditioning?

Social conditioning refers to the impact that society has on your life as a whole. While social conditioning focuses more on your social status in terms of income, living conditions, etc., its scope can go beyond that. Your society can and does influence your beliefs and religion. You may not be a direct practitioner of those beliefs, but you are indirectly affected by them. In certain cultures, certain days are considered sacred. That means that conducting business on those days may be considered an offense. But since we have already discussed religion in the previous chapter, let's look at other aspects of social conditioning that can be easily influenced by dark psychology.

Vulnerability in Advanced Societies

There is a general misconception that being part of a more advanced society makes you impervious to the influences of culture. And I understand that kind of reasoning - how can a society that gave birth to people like Albert Einstein and Neil Armstrong be impacted by something as ridiculous as culture, right?

Well, you're wrong on that score. If anything, you're even more vulnerable, and I'll explain that in a moment.

The Impact of Technology

The biggest advance our society has made today is in the area of technology. We live in a world where things are done instantly. Monetary transactions are completed at the push of a button. An entrepreneur can close a deal in China, motivate his team in South America, guide his partner through a crisis at home and deliver an impressive marketing presentation in Dubai, all before the morning is over, just by pressing a few buttons. This is the world we live in today. If you're putting together a business plan in this era, your products and services must match the same speed we're used to, or else you're setting yourself up to fail. And this is a very good thing. Because I'm pretty sure no one misses the good old days when it took a whole month to get a letter from across the country or three puffs of black smoke shot into the sky to tell you that your loved one loves you back. No. We appreciate the pace at which things are done today.

Vulnerability to Quick Wealth Schemes

Unfortunately, this speed that characterizes our daily lives makes us vulnerable to get-rich-quick schemes. We hear all these amazing stories of people who became millionaires overnight and, on some subconscious level, we desire the same. Some people have exploited these desires to their advantage with what we now know as Ponzi schemes. Named after the infamous Charles Ponzi, a Ponzi scheme is a diabolical way of carrying out daylight robbery with the full consent of the victim. Fraudsters invent a fictitious company that promises large investment returns. After the victim makes an initial commitment, he is rewarded with "returns" that lure him further into the trap the perpetrators have set, causing him to invest more funds. To maximize his profits, the victim is manipulated to bring in more friends to make investments. The more friends he brings, the higher his returns. This builds a pyramid of investors who all put their funds into this company that does not exist. In reality, what the scammers are doing is simply robbing Peter to pay Paul. And then they pay themselves as well. This continues until one day, the company simply disappears into thin air leaving many victims stranded and without their initial investment or returns.

The Role of Social Conditioning

The only logical explanation we can give for a situation like this, where a company with barely any recorded documentation of its existence comes in and rips off hard working people who are generally intelligent in their dealings, is social conditioning. It happened in the 1800's, it happened in the 1900's and it still happens to this day. And despite the knowledge of its existence, people still fall for Ponzi schemes. It's as if we are programmed to do so. And it's not restricted to one class of people. Rich and poor alike fall for it. That tells us that the perpetrator is taking advantage of something that these two classes of people have in common, which is the desire to make more money and make that money fast.

The Role of the Community

But it doesn't end there. To commit this crime successfully, they rely on our sense of community. You are more likely to patronize a company's services or products if you received a direct recommendation from someone you trust rather than recommendations from a random stranger. If your sister shows up saying she made a certain amount of money on an investment and shows you proof of it, instinctively, your trust leads you to base your decision almost entirely on her referral. And when you get your own payout, you automatically become a brand ambassador. This leads you to spread your own news to others in your network and the chain continues. This is very human behavior and many manipulators would capitalize on this. As soon as they get what they need, they disappear or are consumed by their greed and get caught.

Influence of Social Networks

You could argue that this scenario is not likely to happen to you because you are too smart for this, so let me bring it closer to home using the technology we go to bed and wake up to every day. Social media is the craze of our time. People have become "overnight sensations" thanks to social media platforms like YouTube, Instagram, Twitter and Facebook, among others. This has led some of us to nurture similar dreams, but until that happens, we are willing to settle for the "likes" and comments we receive. The problem is that our natural desire to connect with people can become somewhat obsessive if the focus is on our virtual relationships on social networks. This becomes a disturbing thought process where a person's sense of accomplishment will be equated with the number of likes, followers and comments they can get from a post.

Consequences of the Focus on Social Approval

People who start thinking this way stop paying attention to their real relationships. Instead, they lead false and pretentious lives just to gain approval that, in a sad way, validates their daily lives. In their quest for relevance, they emotionally deprive themselves and subject themselves to the sometimes cruel and disapproving opinions of others. This type of behavior has been linked to an increase in suicidal behavior in people who use social networks. It is quite ironic that social networks, which were designed to help us connect with others and build our network, have broken many people because of their dark influences.

Conclusion

In short, social conditioning has a profound impact on our daily lives and makes us susceptible to manipulation through dark psychology. Whether in get-rich-quick schemes or seeking validation in social networks, social and technological influences can be exploited to deceive and control us. Recognizing these vulnerabilities and educating ourselves about the tactics used by manipulators can help us better protect ourselves and make more informed decisions.

Ambition and Personal Aspirations

"Great ambition is the passion of a great character. Those endowed with it can perform very good or very bad acts. It all depends on the principles that guide them."
- Napoleon Bonaparte.

The Nature of Ambition

We all have a to-do list. Sometimes, this list is just a group of tasks designed to help us get through the day. And sometimes, it's a roadmap to where we'd like to be in the near future. For example, your grocery list gets you through the day by getting you what you need to make dinner and possibly the basic essentials that help you become a better member of society (regular soap keeps bad smells at bay and society thanks you). But, putting together a business plan for your startup is a whole different ballgame. You're trying to prepare yourself financially for the future and possibly provide a product or service that positively impacts people's lives. In today's terminology, we call it "boss moves."

Ambition as a Driver of Achievement

Ambition is what drives you towards the goals you have set for yourself. You want something? You strive to achieve it, and for the most ambitious people, when they achieve their goals, they simply try harder. Ambition is an attractive trait in any human being. The aspiration to be better than you are now often puts you behind the wheel that drives your life. No one wants to be with people who are content to sit on the couch all day doing nothing but eating potato chips and changing the channel. People want to be with someone who is truly excited about the beautiful future they envision for themselves and who is working meticulously to achieve it.

The Danger of Uncontrolled Ambition

However, as attractive as ambition is, when taken to the extreme, it can attract the wrong people into your life because it leaves you open and vulnerable. This may sound like a contradictory statement because ambitious people are described as anything but vulnerable. But, as you will learn in this book, what you allow to consume you gains control over you and, when you have no control, you become vulnerable. In previous chapters, I talked about how predators use their victims' weaknesses against them. With this in mind, you'll agree that ambition is an admirable trait in a person and, as a strength, it can help you navigate your way to success. But as a weakness, it can easily be the architect of your destruction.

Personal Aspirations

Where ambition drives your goals, your personal aspirations, on the other hand, can be considered indicators of your success. There are many similarities between aspirations and ambitions, but the main difference is the magnitude and intensity of the latter. Your ambition might be to move up the management ladder before the end of the year, and your aspiration might be to open up more job opportunities when you reach that position. Ambition is more concrete in its desires, while aspirations are those lofty ideas we nurture to feel better about ourselves. On their own, neither ambition nor aspirations should cause you harm, but when other elements come into play, they can be used to manipulate and deceive you.

Ambition in the Work Environment

Most organizations believe that ambition is one of the most desirable qualities in a potential employee. And this is usually because ambitious people are more willing to do whatever it takes to advance in the company than their seemingly more docile peers. People like this are very focused and one-minded when it comes to carrying out their responsibilities; sometimes without thinking about what it would entail to do so, even if it means stepping on the toes of some colleagues. In certain contexts, this can be a good thing. After all, the workplace and the world in general is not a playground where the rules of what's fair for everyone apply. But this attitude can quickly create a hostile work environment that makes it difficult for employees to thrive. The organization's goals may be consistently met, but at the expense of its employees. However, this is not the immediate danger, although it does not mean that such a situation is not a cause for concern.

Risks of Uncontrolled Ambition

A person who is not in control of his ambition can be persuaded and manipulated to do things that are morally and ethically wrong just to fulfill his objectives. It is people with high ambitions and aspirations who are more likely to fall for manipulative techniques involving blackmail. For example, a young professional with an impeccable reputation and a good position within a company is more likely to do anything to maintain that status quo if he or she is ambitious. Even if the things he is expected to do would further tarnish his reputation if those acts were known.

Manipulation through Ambition

Manipulation is not about physically wielding a large and dangerous axe over a person to force them to do something they would not normally do. It is a game of subterfuge and deception. The manipulator acts as a mirror that captures the victim's desires, ambitions and aspirations and then threatens the realization of that vision by also showing the victim's weakness. The victim is led to falsely believe that her only hope of saving her dreams is to fulfill the manipulator's desires. The stronger the ambition, the more likely the victim is to comply, especially if he or she is convinced that he or she can get away with it.

Related Examples

The acts they could be manipulated to perform could range from undermining the authority figure in their lives, committing an act that could be offensive, or anything else the manipulator has in mind. Let me boil this down to relatable proportions. In all of our relationships with people, there is a measure of trust. No matter how paranoid you may be, even the business relationship you have with your tailor is an indication of some level of trust, as you trust him to help you cover your nakedness without harming you in the process. But, just as there is trust, there is also distrust. But we strive to overcome these feelings in hopes of maintaining the bond/bridge between the people involved.

Conclusion

In short, our aspirations and ambitions are not always about the material things we desire. They are also reflected in our perceptions and expectations of the relationships in our lives. Dark psychology is employed by the predators among us to alter this perception and manipulate it in their favor. Recognizing how our ambitions and aspirations can make us vulnerable and being aware of the tactics used by manipulators can help us better protect ourselves and make more informed decisions.

Emotional Scars

"It has been said, 'time heals everything.' I disagree. The wounds remain. Over time, the mind, protecting its sanity, covers them with scar tissue and the pain diminishes, but never disappears."
- Rose Fitzgerald Kennedy.

Experience and its Scars

One of the greatest residual effects of every experience we have is emotions. They say that, in life, experience is the best teacher. Having spent more than a decade trying to understand human nature, I am inclined to agree. Let me share one of my most memorable travel experiences in recent times. I think it best illustrates the point I am trying to make.

The Lesson of Fire

Every year, I pack my bags and travel to explore places that aren't really tourist spots, but are exotic nonetheless. On this particular trip, I was traveling with a tribe of natives on their annual pilgrimage to pay homage to a particular deity. I was not a worshipper, but they were gracious enough to allow me to travel in their company and observe their routines. At night, as we sat by the campfire enjoying the warm glow in the dark after a good meal, I would listen to them chatting in a language I did not understand. My translator would occasionally chime in when there was a general chuckle or a question directed specifically at me. But for the most part, I just watched. And that's when I saw this little boy, no more than 8 or 9 months old, I think. I can't say for sure at that age. Just that the child was crawling toward the fire. I looked around the campfire, but no one seemed to be paying attention. So I made a move to intercept the child, but was immediately rebuked. All the interpreter told me was that the child was about to learn a valuable lesson.

I was worried. The campfire was not very hot, but some of the logs still had fire and there were embers still glowing. I watched carefully. The boy, fascinated by the small flames, came closer and then stopped. Perhaps the heat of the fire made him hesitate. But then, the brave little boy decided to face the heat and move forward. He stopped at a safe distance and then reached out his hand towards the flame, which he quickly withdrew. His face showed an expression of surprise and I could see his lower lip quiver. I wanted to go to him, but the man next to me must have sensed my intentions because he signaled me to wait. The poor baby's expression changed from pain to one of confusion. It was as if he was telepathically talking to the flame and asking why it hurt. He tried to use his hand again and this time he cried. The men clapped and laughed. A woman, possibly his mother, who must have been close by, quickly picked him up and carried him away.

I was outraged. I asked the translator the purpose of this. The chief, through the translator, responded with words I remember to this day. He said, "It is hard to look at fire from a distance and argue against the eyes that such a glorious thing could also be deadly. Sometimes, the hand must do the convincing when the eyes fail. It's called experience." He went on to assure me that no one would have let anything dangerous happen to the child, but I have a feeling that his definition of dangerous is very different from what I imagine it to be.

The Truth in the Chief's Words

Before we get sidetracked into righteous (and rightly so) indignation about her child care practices, we must not neglect the blunt truth in her words. There are lessons in life that only experience can teach you and every experience leaves an emotional scar.

Reactions from Nunca Más

There are certain experiences in life that promptly induce the "never again" reaction. Those experiences are so deeply etched in our minds that we interpret certain signs as a precursor to the event that frightened us in the first place. And the second we observe these signs, our fight or flight instincts are activated, especially if those experiences represent a threat to us. This predictable pattern of behavior is meant to protect us in times of perceived danger. Think of it as a biological defense against what could cause us harm or that emergency drill your body performs when your brain senses you are in danger.

The Science Behind Emotional Scars

What I have described here is the body's reaction to fear, but fear is not the only emotion that can be triggered by your experiences. There is a wide spectrum of emotions ranging from anger to jealousy that can be triggered by an experience.

A woman in love memorizes the scent of her lover. And every time she perceives that scent, her mood is transformed. Sometimes, it induces joy and on certain occasions, it can trigger lust. If that relationship ends, the scents could induce sadness or anger depending on how bad the breakup was. What I am saying is that emotions are part of the human experience. When we feel a certain way, we act a certain way. Certain events can trigger emotions that cause us to react abnormally. My experience of nearly drowning as a teenager causes me to panic every time I close my eyes under the shower. These reactions are triggered by the emotional scars we carry.

Manipulation through Emotional Scars

Now, let me explain the science of this. When an event occurs, whether good or bad, your brain identifies that incident with a specific emotion. This would explain why something as simple as the smell of freshly baked bread can transport you back to your childhood (if that was your experience).

Many marketing companies and advertising agencies employ this knowledge in their advertising strategy. They try to identify their product with things, experiences or events that they know appeal to you or other people like you (their target demographic). Subconsciously, your brain identifies those activities or experiences with their products or services. To sell a barbecue grill, they don't say, "Hi, here's our awesome barbecue grill. Buy it." Instead, they feed you pictures of a fun family 4th of July backyard barbecue. You'd see happy kids running around, smiling grandparents chatting with a family member and the teens doing something cool. All this interspersed with a nice cut of meat cooking on the grill. It's almost as if they were saying, if you buy this grill, you also buy this experience. In other words, you were visually manipulated into making a purchase.

Emotional Scars and Vulnerability

This is not necessarily sinister per se. But ordinary people we encounter in our daily lives can take advantage of this weakness. If you are easily emotionally swayed, you can be manipulated into making impulsive decisions on anything from an impulse purchase to falling in love with people on emotional principles alone. People can disguise themselves and pass themselves off as something they are not. They wear clothes and perfumes that make it look like they are wealthy, and because you have a strong emotional connection to wealth, you overlook other warning signs and make a regrettable decision. Whether good or bad, your emotional scars can make you vulnerable to deception and manipulation.

CHAPTER IV: RECOGNIZING AND IDENTIFYING YOUR REALITY
Accepting the Lies We Tell Ourselves

"Above all, do not lie to yourself. The man who lies to himself and listens to his own lie comes to the point where he cannot distinguish the truth within him or around him, and so loses all respect for himself and for others. And having no respect, he ceases to love."
- Fyodor Dostoyevsky.

The Danger of Personal Lies

There are many forms of lies that we hear every day. Sometimes, lies are told to protect you from something. It could be something as trivial as keeping knowledge of something you're not ready to know, like a surprise birthday party. Sometimes, lies are more complicated, but not told entirely out of malice, like telling a person about your cheating spouse. The point is, for better or worse, we all tell lies, but no lie is more serious than the lies we tell ourselves. There is more danger in the lies we tell ourselves than in the lies other people tell us (this will be discussed at length in the next chapter) and here's why.

Biological Defense and Self-Deception

In the previous chapter, I talked about the body's biological defense when the brain detects danger or situations that threaten us. These impulses, however irrational they may seem, are meant to protect us. Lying to ourselves dulls these instincts and exposes us to potential dangers. It's like seeing a speeding car coming down the road and deciding to cross anyway. Instinctively, your body knows that this situation is precarious. A small miscalculation could result in a fatal accident. But instead of waiting for the car to pass, you convince yourself that you are faster than the car, or that the car is farther away than it looks, or that it is not going as fast as it seems. These are the kind of lies we tell ourselves.

Common Forms of Self-Deception

Self-deception occurs in many forms. But the most popular form of self-deception is denial. We convince ourselves that the threat is not real or imminent, so we make risky decisions that we quickly regret. Denial is not always a clear case of admitting that something does or does not exist. Sometimes, it masquerades as optimism in a very serious situation. And in some cases, the opposite is true. You are in a good situation, but you choose to be pessimistic and deny the possibilities. According to one school of thought, humans are more susceptible to self-deception because we choose to hold on to certain beliefs. Say, for example, you meet an amazing person who seems to meet all your criteria for relating to someone. But underneath that layer, you may feel a reluctance or even know clearly that you are being deceived, but instead of acting on that instinct, you choose to act on the hope that people can be what they appear to be.

Examples of Negation

We hear the expression "wolf in sheep's clothing" all the time. There is no doubt that the wolf can be very good at disguising itself as a sheep, just as there is no doubt that the sheep at a primal level were aware of the wolf in their midst, but chose to deny the existence of the threat because they wanted to believe that the wolf was one of them. We can all imagine how that story unfolded. This pattern of behavior over time dampens the alarms that sound in our senses whenever a crisis arises because of what we tell ourselves.

Rationalization

After denial is rationalization. Denial and rationalization are tools of the same trade. They work together in self-deception. Rationalization is essentially how you explain the situation. I've had female friends (and some male friends in the same situation) who are in a relationship that isn't really healthy for them, but instead of ending things by taking themselves out of the equation, somehow they always seem to find more reasons to stay in that relationship. Women in abusive relationships know that a man who raises his hand against you is showing the highest form of disrespect.

But I have heard these violent men describe themselves as caring and their occasional violence as one of their ways of showing the woman they care. This behavior doesn't just apply to relationships.

Self-deception at Work

People have found themselves working at a place they know is exploiting them. But they tell themselves how hard it is to find work and how they wouldn't be able to pay the bills if they left. And so they continue to work under these terrible conditions, refusing even to protest because they have come to accept the situation as normal thanks to their rationalizations and denials.

Sad Lives and Self-Deception

Whether in our careers or in our normal relationships, many of us lead sad and unfulfilled lives because we have convinced ourselves that we cannot do otherwise and that this is our destiny. Some people even go a step further and say that they deserve what they are getting because of some fault committed in the past. In other words, they have chosen to open the doors of their own cells, lock themselves in and then act as jailers. Self-deception is a mental prison of sorts, but it also has its merits.

Merits of Self-Deception

When faced with challenges that threaten to overwhelm us, a little self-deception can help build your confidence and level the playing field. You can choose a more positive phrase other than self-deception to describe it, but it doesn't change what it is. People like to call it pep talk, pep talk, or giving themselves a morale boost...whatever you choose to call it, it boils down to convincing yourself of something you're not. A man who wants to get close to a very beautiful woman he feels is out of his league has to convince himself that he is all that. He acts more confident than he really feels to convince himself that he is really confident. So, you see, self-confidence can go both ways. But to avoid falling victim to people who use elements of dark psychology to get their way, you need to recognize the truth for what it is.

Conclusion

If your instincts are activated, instead of denying it, ask questions. Find out why you feel the way you do about the person and try to get more answers. When you learn to trust your instincts, you can better protect yourself. If a situation is not working out favorably for you, instead of choosing to be powerless about it (because yes, it is a choice), you should actively seek a way out of the situation. Don't lie to yourself. The truth may not be what we want it to be, but you shouldn't have to live a painful lie just to deny it. Recognize the lies you tell yourself for what they really are.

Ignore the Lies Others Tell Us

"Lies and secrets...are like a cancer in the soul. They consume what is good and leave only destruction behind."
- Cassandra Clare.

The Destructive Nature of Lies

We have all been victims of lies at some point in our lives. That doesn't mean that everyone who came into our circle and lied to us was trying to use us to carry out some evil plan. In fact, there are truths that, when told with malicious intent, can have the same effect as a terrible lie, if not worse. Whether the lies come from your best friend, a parent or even someone at work, the effect can be devastating. In some cases, it's not the lie itself that hurts. It's the knowledge that someone you trusted made a deliberate decision to fabricate a story and convince you it's real. Certain lies are told simply by not saying anything about it. People think, "If I didn't say anything, I didn't lie." But in reality, that's called a lie of omission.

The Web of Lies

It is almost impossible to start with a single lie and leave it at that. One lie leads to another, which leads to yet another, until both the person lying and the person being lied to are caught in a web of lies. This web can be so tangled that untangling the truth becomes impossible. Lies have a way of changing you, and that change is not always good. This is because you are being fed a fabricated version of reality. Against our better judgment, we believe these lies and the anger we feel when the truth is revealed is not directed solely at the liar in question. We blame ourselves for believing these lies.

Loss of Faith and Distrust

When we discover that we are being lied to, we react not only to the person and what they represent, but our identity is also questioned. Your loss of faith is not only in the person, but in yourself as well. Loss of faith results in doubt. And doubts lead to distrust. But before we dive into the effect of lies, let's explore why we fall for lies in the first place.

The Desire to Believe

I'm going to start with the general population and then bring things closer to home. If you have been active online, you will notice that the most read and followed stories are the sensationalist pieces. In recent times, there has been an increase in the spread of stories that have no truth to them whatsoever. Even the prestigious Rolling Stone magazine, known for its excellent reporting skills, published a story (which they believed to be true) that turned out to be false. So, you ask yourself, how is it possible that people with years of skills and experience could fall for that kind of lie? If you're expecting some grand revelation of the truth, I'm sorry to disappoint you. The reason is quite simple and naturally a very human answer. They wanted to believe it.

Confirmation of Personal Beliefs

In the same way, we fall for the lies we are told because we want to believe they are true. This happens on several levels and is not always related to people who are very close to us. For example, if you share a certain political opinion or view, you are more likely to follow or read articles or publications that support your belief. If someone tells a lie that supports your belief, you are more inclined to fall for that lie because you want it to confirm your own personal beliefs or theories. This also applies in our relationships. You believe that love should be a certain way and because a person shows patterns that correspond with your idea of what love is, you choose to ignore the other warning signs and believe their lies instead.

Self-Interest and Self-Deception

Another reason we believe a lie is because we have a vested interest in the lie. A manipulator presents you with an alternative reality that you suspect is false, but because your own self-interest conflicts with the truth, you choose to accept the lie instead. The self-interest may not just be about personal gain. It could be your special feelings for the person. You like the person and have created a halo around them. So, you'd rather cling to your idealized version of events (self-deception in action here) than face the possible reality that this person may be more sinister than they appear and that their ulterior motives may not be for your own benefit at all.

Lies that Alter Reality and Self Image

Lies that come from an altered reality of events are not the only type of lies that can be used to manipulate us. When we think of being lied to, we focus more on events that were fabricated for the benefit of the liar, but there are other types of lies that can be just as vicious, if not more so. I'm referring to lies that are told to change your perception of yourself. Throughout each chapter of this book, I have strongly emphasized that we are most vulnerable when our emotions are at the forefront. Especially when those emotions are out of control. When a manipulator encounters a person who seems emotionally stable, he knows that it would be difficult to work his wicked charms on such a person. So his first line of action is to wear down that person's emotional base.

Undermining Self-Esteem

They look for chinks in the person's proverbial armor and begin to exploit them. Let's say you're normally a confident person, but you have some insecurities about your body. A master manipulator would take advantage of that concern and twist it around by amplifying your fears. It may not be perceived as a direct insult, but it would be used strategically to imply that the problem is worse than it really is. Derogatory comments about how big you look today or how you need to cut back on carbs are subtle but effective insinuations of the problem they hope to amplify. When you begin to accept these lies, you'll find yourself reflecting on problems that really aren't problems in the first place. And gradually, the proverbial mote becomes a mountain and you find yourself buried under insecurities that have eaten away at your confidence until you are exactly what the manipulator wants you to be: a person with low self-esteem and low confidence who can be easily manipulated.

Manipulation Through Positive and Negative Reinforcement

If undermining your self-esteem does not yield the desired results, they try the negative route. I want to tell you that you can't do something and use your past experiences and emotions to support this lie until you believe it. Sometimes, the opposite happens. They lull you into a state where you feel safe, even though the reality is different. This tactic is often used when the perpetrator wants to extract something like money or a favor from you. They use positive reinforcement rooted in lies to give you a false sense of security and then attack. It takes mental clarity and effort to see through the lies people tell in whatever form they appear.

Conclusion

To avoid falling into the trap of the lies others tell us, we must be vigilant and cultivate a clear understanding of reality. Recognizing our emotional vulnerabilities and maintaining a critical mind will help us navigate the complexities of human relationships and protect us from manipulation.

Don't Obsess About The Past

"I have learned that, if you must leave a place where you have lived and loved and where all your yesterdays are buried deep, leave it in any way but a slow way. Leave it as fast as you can. Never look back and never believe that an hour you remember is better because it is dead. The years past seem safe, conquered, while the future lives in a cloud, formidable from a distance."
- Beryl Markham.

Keep your eyes on the present

In a track race, athletes are trained to stay focused and rooted in the present. They don't look back, figuratively or literally. Their senses are tuned to the moment. When the race starts, it's all about them, the track and the finish line. That's because, the second they start paying attention to something other than the race, they start to lose. Even in a relay race, where the athlete has to look back and take the baton from their partner, their gaze quickly returns to the track in front of them as soon as the baton changes hands. Life is like a race and looking back at the past can distract you and stop you from being the best you can be. More importantly, this kind of distraction is the kind of thing a manipulator would use against you.

The Danger of Reliving the Past

When the brain is not actively activating emotions that come from memories, our mind does an excellent job of bringing all those emotions to the forefront. I tried to think of how to best explain the firm grip our past can have on us and a scene from one of my favorite movies illustrates this. Without going into the plot of the movie [Titans of the Pacific], let me set the scene for you. Mako and Raleigh are paired up to test the Jaeger [a machine designed to destroy aliens] for the first time and, in order to manipulate the machine, there must be a mental connection through what they call the mind link. The connection process takes you through a series of memories [your past] before rooting you in the present. Mako's memory of his past is so vivid that he gets stuck in it. This results in his disconnection from present reality. This disconnection almost results in the activation of a nuclear weapon that could have destroyed the present. Returning to us, our reconnection with our past may not be as vivid, but the psychological threat posed by obsessing over the past is just as potent.

Ruminating: A Psychological Trap

When we talked about emotional scarring in the past, we explored the pain/emotions triggered by events and focused on our biological defense mechanisms. We know that the brain interprets certain signs in our environment as threats and, in doing so, triggers reactions that we cannot always control. This is somewhat similar, except this time we are actively engaging a negative experience by constantly thinking about it. And in the process, we unleash a flood of emotions that may overwhelm us. Psychologists refer to this as rumination. Just as a goat [or a cow] regurgitates the food it ate hours earlier and chews it up, we tend to regurgitate our experiences and obsess over them.

The Illusion of Security of the Past

But we don't just hold on to the negative past, sometimes the past has many positive memories that bring us comfort. This makes it hard to let go. Unfortunately, it is just as easy to become disillusioned with the positive past as it is with the negative past. We all know someone in our life who is fond of using the phrase "the good old days" and we know how heartbreaking it can be to see them clinging to the remnants of the so-called glory days. You may not use that phrase, but your fondness for the past can quickly get you stuck in that memory and set you on a path that destroys your opportunities in the present.

The Deception of Good Memories

Of course, you can argue that if bad memories evoke bad emotions, then good memories evoke good emotions and that can't be bad. The truth is, as long as it disconnects you from present reality, it is bad. And this is what dark psychology exploits. When you live your life in the past, you become rooted in a situation that either slows you down or stops you from moving forward. Fear is one of the most powerful emotions that our memories can trigger. And it's not just the famous fear of the bogeyman [or whatever it is that inspires fear in you] that holds you back. Fear of uncertainty can also hold you back. You might be holding on to a relationship, job or lifestyle simply because you're afraid of what will happen if that thing or person is no longer in your life. And that fear keeps you there, even when the situation is not ideal for you.

The Fear of Uncertainty and Exploitation

This is not denial because you are aware of the wrongness of the situation. You have simply decided to focus your attention on what was and distance yourself or, worse, accept what is because you are afraid of what will/could be. And you must believe that the manipulators and saboteurs in your life will capitalize on this fear and work their evil to exploit this knowledge until they get what they want. Their modus operandi would be to somehow strengthen the hold this past has on you and convince you that the present reality is a necessity. They use your insistence on focusing on the past to discredit your present and rob you of a future. The irony here is that you are at least partially aware of what is happening, but you have made a conscious or subconscious decision to exclude yourself from the equation and justify your decision with an event that has already happened.

The Illusion of Lack of Choice

In essence, you yourself have created this illusion of no choice and have handed over the reins of your present to others. This is not to say that looking back is completely wrong. Rear-view mirrors were created specifically for this purpose. The point here is, if you really want to separate the truth from the lies, staying rooted in the present is one way to do it. Psychologists say that people who obsess about the past are more likely to be depressed than others. Depression is one of those dark emotions that leaves you vulnerable. And if you seek treatment for depression, one of the steps to overcoming it is to step back into the past, accept the reality of the situation and then apply the lessons learned from the past revisited before letting it go.

Control of the Present

If you are having trouble letting go, you just need to remind yourself that you have absolutely no control over what has happened. No matter how much you revisit it and obsess over it, you cannot change what has happened. The same can be said of the future. There are many possibilities. Sure, the steps you take now might determine to some extent what will happen tomorrow, but there are too many variables to predict the future accurately. What you own and have total control over is what you do now. Disconnect from the past and the fears of the future and put your focus on the "now".

Blind Optimism

The Nature of Optimism

When we take on responsibilities in life, we do so with enthusiasm and energy. And, like everything else in life, we encounter challenges that can range from mild obstacles to raging storms that seem destined for our destruction. At such times, our enthusiasm and energy can wane. What keeps us from giving up and helps us get through those difficult times is optimism. But there are different levels of optimism and not all have the same positive impact on our lives. There is a type of optimism that seems to disconnect us from reality and that type of optimism is known as blind optimism. But before we delve into that, let's examine that aspect of human nature that makes us want to believe in an alternative outcome even when we face a very difficult situation. Like the author of the above quote, we are interested in what makes us unshakable in the face of darkness.

Optimism: An Intrinsic Part of Being Human

Like all facets of human emotional behavior, we seem to be simply hard-wired to be optimistic. And it's not just in the face of danger. This behavior is present in our simple everyday activities. You have a product that is perhaps a few days past its expiration date, but you decide to consume it anyway in the hope that it won't cause you harm. Or you approach a traffic light just as it changes color and, instead of braking, you speed up in the hope of passing without getting caught. Or you even risk asking a person out in the hope that they will feel the same way about you, rather than seeing your feelings exposed and crushed. It's part of your emotional reflex. Despite Murphy's Law, you're optimistic because you're human.

The Danger of Blind Optimism

However, some people take this optimistic approach to their dealings a bit too far. Instead of simply pushing the envelope, as I illustrated with the examples above, they put absolute faith in the possibility that the good outcome they hope for will outweigh the likelihood of things going wrong. This type of thinking inspires reckless behavior that could have a painful ending if the emotion goes unchecked. Being optimistic has many health and mental benefits. If you have ever read the book The Power of Positive Thinking by Norman Vincent, you will no doubt be aware of how well positive thinking can serve you. Medical studies show that optimistic people are more likely to recover from life-threatening illnesses than people who are the opposite. However, optimism can blind you.

The Self-Deception of Blind Optimism

Blind optimism is a form of self-deception. In this case, you are not just thinking that you have a good chance of getting the desired positive outcome. You have deluded yourself into thinking that things will unfold the way you expect and, because you are relying on the positive aspects of the situation, you do not take steps to protect yourself in case things go wrong because you are not even considering any negative notions. When you are blinded by optimism, you have a greater tendency to rationalize and explain the reality of the situation. Even when you are presented with the gravity of the situation, your blind optimism prevents you from taking any action that might mitigate the negative outcomes.

Blind Optimism and Disconnection from Reality

As I mentioned earlier, we fall into a lie because we want to. Blind optimism is a type of lie that also works by distancing us from the reality of things. You find yourself confronting a lie directly in the face, but perhaps because accepting the reality that this person or situation is not what it seems may be too painful, we flip the optimism switch up a little higher. Our need to want to believe that people are not as terrible as they can be makes us give in to demands that have a negative impact on us. Then, we replace that negative instinct with a glowing reaction straight out of the pages of the book of blind optimism. And many times, we do this because we want to feel good about the situation or the person.

Consequences of Blind Optimism

Blind optimism affects your ability to accurately assess the pitfalls and problem areas in any given situation. It puts you in a state of mind where you are almost walking on clouds and gives you a false sense of security. You feel invincible in the face of risks and take no precautions. The upside of blind optimism is that you are more likely to take risks than most. In business, people who are blindly optimistic are often in the category of early adopters. When a new product hits the market, while others are busy calculating the risks and trying to assess its likelihood, these guys dive in head first. Many new companies rely on people like these.

The Daily Reality of Blind Optimism

In everyday life, blind optimism creates a dangerous disconnect from reality. It's like a person who wakes up in the morning and decides he wants to parachute. Without thinking about altitudes, weather conditions or the landscape, they simply strap on the parachute and jump. The odds of hitting a rock before you can deploy your parachute are as high as hitting the ground in one piece. But they chose to prepare only for the reality they are willing to accept. You can't deal with people the same way and not expect some kind of negative reaction. There is ignorance and then there is the willingness to see the danger ahead and choose to do nothing about it. It doesn't matter if this person is your best friend, your mother or your partner. If you see the signs that could imply something else is at stake, wishing and hoping you're wrong won't protect you if you're right. Sure, it might temporarily keep that relationship in a good place, but in the long run, even that too will disintegrate. Taking the blindfold off would require you to be honest with yourself.

The Truth Hurts, but it Frees

There is a common saying that the truth is bitter. I wish I could say that this is not true. When it comes to your relationships with people, bitter is an understatement in describing the truth. Confronting the reality of the situation can generate pain you never imagined and, for a while, it's going to hurt. In a situation where your emotions are being taken advantage of, you can't afford to bury your head in the sand because you don't want to face the reality of your experience. Even a gradual disclosure is not helpful. What you need to do is rip off the blindfold at once and face the emotions head on. The truth hurts, but it will also set you free. You just need to remind yourself that all this pain is part of the process and that the pain brings you one step closer to healing.

The Vicious Cycle

"Once you think things are permanent, you're trapped in a world without doors."
- Genesis P. Orridge.

The Four Walls of Deception

The four walls that imprison us in a web of deception are the lies we tell ourselves, the lies others tell us, anchoring ourselves in the past and blind optimism. Each of these is a facet of the false realities that trap us and, on their own, can have a terrible impact on us. However, when all of these elements work together, the results can be devastating. People who have escaped or lived a life where they were constantly manipulated can identify at least three of these elements at work when the manipulations were at their peak.

The Beginning of the Deception

As with all forms of deception, it all begins with a lie. The lie is not easily discernible at first. Perhaps, on an instinctive level, you feel that something is not right, but there is nothing concrete to base your feelings on, so you decide to accept the lie. The decision to accept the lie doesn't always happen on its own. You don't just accept the lie. On a personal level, you have to convince yourself to believe the lie, and this usually requires you to lie to yourself. You tell yourself that it's not as bad as it seems. You tell yourself that the person has no reason to lie to you. Basically, you tell yourself anything you need to convince yourself that your instincts are wrong.

The Blindness of Optimism

To give substance to the lie you are telling yourself, you add a good dose of unrealistic expectations under the guise of being optimistic. This optimism further damages your good judgment and leaves you even more vulnerable than you were initially. And to remove any doubt, you turn to a past experience to validate your present choices, and things go downhill from there. The situation doesn't always play out this way. Sometimes, one thing comes before the other, but the goal is the same: to trap and deceive you.

The Manipulator as Puppeteer

When this cycle is in play, the manipulator becomes the puppeteer and you become the puppet. The strings with which they manipulate you are your emotions. They shake you to do their will. It is important to remember that one person's ability to successfully manipulate another does not make them a diabolical master planner. These events often unfold according to a natural order of things. When you leave something of value outside your home and a thief comes and steals it, you can't say he planned the incident. By nature, these people have been trained to be takers. Whether they have the owner's consent or not, they are inclined to simply take, especially when the opportunity presents itself. In the same way, a manipulator is inclined to use the emotions of others against them for their own personal gain. Emotions are to a manipulator what a wand is to a magician. And they use them to their advantage.

The Power of Emotions

There is a wide spectrum of emotions that the average human being experiences. And knowing that emotions are the tools that manipulators use to exploit us might make you instinctively want to turn off your emotions. And I can relate to that line of thinking. But the truth is that numbing your emotions could have an adverse negative effect. For starters, numbing your emotions could lead you to seek escape in other places like drugs and alcohol, which give you the illusion of not feeling when they actually amplify your feelings. Furthermore, the decision to numb your emotions [if such a thing were possible] would mean not experiencing the good stuff as well. Because while you want to get rid of negative emotions like greed, anger and sadness, you also want to experience joy, happiness and peace. Emotions are some of the things that make our existence as humans more valuable and getting rid of these emotions would be like living in a world without color. Instead of trying to numb these emotions, we can exercise more control over them and use them to help us grow as individuals.

The Great Deception: Lack of Control

This brings us to the next important issue: control. Although manipulators work our emotions against us, their greatest weapon is to make us believe that we have no control. This grand illusion makes us think that we are powerless and helpless and that there is nothing we can do about it. But if you go through this section of the book, even if you go back to the beginning, you will notice something very interesting. The common denominator in all of this is you, and in order for their plans to work, some kind of consent on your part is required. I'm not saying that what has happened or is happening is your fault. Not at all. All I am trying to say is that you are not as helpless as you seem. One of the reasons I wrote this book is to help those who are under the influences of dark psychology to escape and overcome its hold. And the first step in doing so is to embrace the powers you have. Your emotions can make you vulnerable, but with the right application of knowledge, your emotions can become your greatest ally in this battle.

Embracing your Emotions

You have a choice and you have a voice. Don't let anyone convince you otherwise. In the next chapter, we'll delve into how to break free from it all. Right now, I want you to look inward as if you were looking in a mirror. Embrace your emotions: the fear, the anger, the pain. They are all part of you. They may not paint a perfect picture, but for a moment, put your expectations of perfection on the shelf. Focus on what you're feeling right now. Whether those emotions are good or bad, make the decision to want something better for yourself. The heavens won't open, there won't be celestial music playing somewhere in the sky, and your situation won't change overnight. On the contrary, things could get worse before they get better. But when you make this decision, you are mentally preparing yourself for what is to come.

The Need for Change

If you need a more tangible reason to drive this sudden transformation from what you have come to accept as your comfort zone, remind yourself that you are reason enough to make it happen. You deserve better, your opinions matter and there is no other person more powerful and instrumental in influencing this change you desire than yourself. Up to this point, you have taken care of others. You adapted your needs to meet the expectations of others, you let go of your sense of self to accommodate the needs of others and for a long time, you've been on the back shelf and lost value. But no more. Now it's time to look out for your own interests and there's no shame in that. That negative voice or manipulator in your life will want to tell you that you are being selfish. Counter this obvious lie with the truth. The truth is that your ability to care and look out for others begins with the decision to care for yourself first. Therefore, being "selfish" right now is the best step you can take toward being selfless.

In short, the vicious cycle of lies, blind optimism and anchoring yourself in the past creates a trap of emotional manipulation that can be devastating. However, recognizing these dynamics and taking control of your emotions is the first step to freeing yourself and breaking this destructive cycle.

CHAPTER V: HOW TO BREAK FREE
Accepting That You Have A Problem

"Often, it's not about becoming a new person, it's about becoming the person you were meant to be and already are, but don't know how to be."
- Heath L. Buckmaster.

The Reality of Opinions and Self-Perception

Many times, we focus more on the opinion of others: on how the world sees us or how we want the world to see us. The current trend is summarized in the motto: "fake it till you make it". This approach to life leads us to have a fragile and superficial relationship with reality. We become so immersed in pretending that we cannot remove the mask even when we are alone. This form of self-deception can become so deeply rooted in our lives that one day we may wake up to a situation that totally contradicts the false reality we have worked so hard to preserve, which sometimes surprises and hurts us deeply.

Breaking Illusions

If we are completely honest, we are not always surprised by the lies we are told. On some level, we know that. What takes us by surprise is how much it hurts us. And it is this pain that makes us avoid the problem in the first place. To break free, the first step is to confront the situation and break any illusions. You can't move forward if you don't break the illusions that surround you. Arm yourself with the knowledge that you have a choice. Then, make the conscious decision to see things as they are. That deal that seems too good to be true probably is.

Trusting your Instincts

Next, trust your instincts. There are times when a lie has been so skillfully fabricated that it seems true. But, on a gut level, you may feel an imbalance between what should be, what is, and what is projected to you. There may be no physical signs that something is wrong, but you sense that something is wrong. At times like that, it's easy to ignore those feelings and go along with what you're being told. You may not want to appear rude or be perceived in a certain way, so you give in and ignore that inner voice.

Learning to trust your instincts takes practice over time. Start by training yourself on small, simple things. Maybe you're about to leave the house and you feel the need to double-check something. Or maybe you think of someone and feel the need to call them. These are small instances and may not lead to big rewards, but they build your trust in your instincts so that when situations of real importance arise, you can better discern what your instincts are telling you and act accordingly. If you are already in a situation and don't have time to train your ability to trust your instincts, don't lose hope. Your instincts are there to protect you. And as long as you are alive, your instincts will want to help you stay alive. In this situation, you just want to get out of it.

Asking the Right Questions

So what are your instincts telling you? That question will lead you to the next step: asking the right questions. Start with yourself. Try to figure out why you feel the way you feel. Look at your current situation, find out why you are no longer happy with how you feel. Ask yourself why you feel this way and try to be more specific about your feelings. I said that emotions make you vulnerable, but they can also act as a guide when you feel lost.

When you cannot satisfactorily provide the answers you seek, look outside yourself. Looking outside yourself does not necessarily mean confronting the predator, although it may eventually come to this. I don't recommend going the direct route right away, as you will give the perpetrator the opportunity to present a defense that may further cloud your judgment and not get the results you want. It may also alert the person that you are aware of their intentions, triggering their own fight or flight response.

Instead, turn to people within your circle of trust. Since you're trying to navigate through a situation that involves a breach of trust, it can be difficult to decide who to suddenly trust. If you're really concerned about that, go to someone who has little or no personal stake in the equation. Someone who is not directly related to you or the person or persons involved might be the best choice. These people are more likely to be honest with you.

Listen to the answers

When you ask the questions, the next most important thing is to listen to the answers. This may sound somewhat unbelievable because, of course, you're going to listen to the answers. The reality is that our self-deception can make us selective about the answers we get. We tell ourselves that we are listening, but we are only paying attention to the answers we want to hear rather than the answers we are actually getting. You may have shattered the illusions around you, but there is still a part of you that clings to the comfort those illusions provide. The pain of confronting the reality of the situation would deter you from listening to the real answers to the questions you have asked.

Processing New Information

Listening really requires some sense of detachment, but not from reality this time. You need to detach from your emotions. This detachment from your emotions will lead you to the next step, which is to process the new information logically. Acting irrationally can complicate situations more than they already are. Letting all the emotions build up and rise to the surface makes your exit strategy much more difficult. The irrational part of you, when confronted with the truth, may want everything to go to hell. Your anger, which is justified, may prompt you to take actions that help calm your emotions in the short term. But in the long run, you might regret those actions. I'm not saying deny your emotions, I'm saying don't act based on those emotions. First, address the situation and then your emotions.

Conclusion

Accepting that you have a problem is the first step toward liberation. By facing the situation honestly, trusting your instincts, asking the right questions, truly listening to the answers and processing the new information logically, you can begin to break the cycle of manipulation and deception that traps you. This process will not be easy or quick, but it is critical to regaining your freedom and autonomy.

Act Fast

"It's the action, not the fruit of the action that matters. You have to do the right thing. It may not be in your power, it may not be in your time that there will be any fruit. But that doesn't mean you stop doing the right thing. You may never know what results come from your action. But if you do nothing, there will be no result."
- Mahatma Gandhi.

Confront Reality

You have faced the reality of your situation and that is usually the most difficult step. However, it doesn't end there. You can't expect the situation to go away on its own. Remember, you have a choice in this. Even your inaction is a deliberate choice you have made and, as the great Mahatma Gandhi said, if you do nothing, there will be no results. Freeing yourself from a web of delusion can be exciting at first until you have to deal with the flood of emotions that follows. The intensity of the emotions can make us want to go into denial. And this is a normal process. In the five stages of grief, the first stage is denial. The longer you take to act, the deeper and faster your denial will settle in. And when denial sets in, there is a high probability that you will return to the vicious cycle that characterized this stage of your life. Avoid this by taking quick action now. It doesn't have to be something grandiose. Something as simple as informing your close friend about the reality of the situation can set in motion a series of events that will eventually set you free.

Breaks the Fabric of Illusion

After making the decision to act, you should know that the fabric of the illusion is made of a stronger material than glass. Although I used the term "breaking your illusion," what is really happening is a gradual separation of fact from fiction. With your emotions in overdrive, the illusion may be working its way back into your heart using fragments of your emotions to repair it. When a liar is caught in a lie, they may try to recruit others to reinforce that lie when they feel they no longer have control over you. A deceitful partner you have recently broken up with may, at this point, try to use mutual relationships to influence you to change your mind.

The person they use may not be in cahoots with them, they are simply manipulated to do what they do. Liars have no problem using friends, family and even religious leaders to get what they want. You have to stand up for the choice you have made and decide to see this through to the end.

Overcome Emotional Gambles

When the attempt to manipulate you through other people fails, the next thing they do is resort to their old method which is to cling to your own emotions. In divorce situations, spouses use their partner's emotional concern for their children to bring them down. They use threats like "if you leave, you'll never see the kids again" to try to maintain control. In business, there is usually an implied threat to cut the other person off without any payoff. This is a last-ditch effort on the part of the manipulator to try to control their victim. They know that their charms are no longer effective and, feeling threatened by their loss of control, they use power plays like this to try to gain the upper hand. Power plays usually involve forms of blackmail ranging from trivial things to deep secrets that were entrusted to them when the relationship was good. The blackmailer may want financial payoffs, more negotiating leverage and, for the most sinister individuals, they simply want control.

Maintain Calm and Clarity

At this point, their actions may have you in a corner making you want to react and vent. I strongly advise you not to do so. You will need both your logic and your instincts if you want to get out of this without further damage. Although the truth of the situation is that when you discover that you have been constantly cheated on, you are left with emotional scars, so the question of getting out of the situation unscathed becomes irrelevant. However, priority should be given to taking the route that allows you to leave that toxic situation without damaging yourself further. Emotionally, you are all over the place. Anger, rage, hurt and disappointment are just the tip of the iceberg. But you need to think logically. Keep your head above water and be alert.

Act with Determination

They say that an animal is most dangerous when it feels cornered. For a human, it is worse. When a person has been caught in the web of deceit they weave, they want to do everything to protect themselves. At that point, their selfish instincts to protect themselves are activated to the max and they are willing to do anything to avoid facing the consequences of their actions. As with human nature, it is not possible to predict how far they are willing to go to avoid this. So, rather than showing them your agenda of bringing them to justice, your priority should be to make sure you are safe. If possible, I would recommend a physical separation, however temporary, from the person you feel is manipulating you. Not only does it give you space to think clearly, but it can also weaken the hold they have over you. Because being in the same proximity, especially if they are in their own territory, can make you more vulnerable to further manipulation.

Keep your Resolution

Many liars and manipulators turn on their charm when they have been caught. They will appear deeply remorseful, apologetic and may even go to extreme lengths to try to convince you of their remorse. But don't be fooled, as this could be just another act and another attempt to manipulate you into taking less drastic measures that they may find unfavorable. If you feel your resolve weakening, at least get out of the situation. That action alone can make all the difference.

Conclusion

Acting quickly is crucial to free yourself from manipulation and deception. Don't let fear, doubt or intense emotions paralyze you. Remember that your safety and well-being are most important. Taking action, even if it is only a small step, can trigger a series of events that will lead you toward freedom and recovery. Keep your logic and instincts in the forefront, and don't be swayed by emotional manipulations or manipulators' attempts to regain control.

How to Free Yourself

"The best way to not feel hopeless is to get up and do something. Don't wait for good things to happen to you. If you go out and make good things happen, you will fill the world with hope, you will fill yourself with hope."
- Barrack Obama.

Breaking the Confusion

When you find yourself trapped by the manipulations of others, one of the emotions you will experience is confusion. This contributes to clouding your rational thinking, leaving you with a sense of helplessness. At this point, you may even be questioning the reality of what you are facing. If you continue to entertain these doubts, it will lead to denial. You will probably come to the conclusion that you have misunderstood certain things and have come to the wrong conclusion. This type of thinking will drive you back into the arms of the manipulator. Resist the temptation to give in by getting a second opinion. In a health crisis, people go to another doctor to get a second opinion. This is to remove any hint of doubt you may have about the first diagnosis and affirm the best course of treatment for you. Likewise, getting another person's opinion can help you discern the truth of the situation and what your next steps might be. Remember, it is best to go to someone who has demonstrated countless times that they have your best interest in mind.

Seeking Help and Support

Now that you have the confirmation you need, don't try to meet the challenge on your own. The situation may not be something you want anyone else to know about. You may worry that people will call you naïve for being in this situation. The truth is, they probably will. But they are entitled to their own opinions. Don't let fear of what people might say ruin your chance to create a better life for yourself. You don't have to prove anything to anyone but yourself. The world can think whatever it wants. Right now, your priority is to get out of the situation and survive long enough to thrive.

Acting decisively

When you have the help you need, the next step is to confront the perpetrator. I suggest you choose the scene or location for this. Choose a location that you know gives you the advantage. This will require careful planning on your part. If the perpetrator exists in the cyber world, you will need to involve the police and relevant authorities, especially if the person scammed you out of money. Do a preliminary investigation on your own. There are software applications that perform facial recognition on popular social networking sites such as Instagram and Facebook. Look for clues about the person's true identity in the conversations you have had and only when you are armed with enough evidence, confront the person.

Facing Reality

If the confrontation occurs before you have evidence, you run the risk of scaring the perpetrator into hiding. Of course, with the authorities involved, they will eventually catch him, but it may take longer than it would normally take if you had patiently prepared yourself before confronting him. If it is someone who lives near you, things may have to be done differently. If you fear for your life in any way, please do not confront this person on your own. In abusive relationships, it is best to avoid confrontations altogether. Simply wait for the right time and look for the best opportunity to escape. Don't give in to demands about having "one last conversation." And if you must consent to such a meeting, make sure you are not alone. Notify the people you care about and have at least one person present during this meeting. Your safety is the priority.

Action Plan for Abusive Situations

If you are in an abusive situation, here's what I advise you to do:

Seek professional help: Call a local organization that serves victims of abuse in your area. This is probably the most important step you will take, as they have professionals who are there to guide and advise you on your next course of action.

2. Escape when you can: Don't wait for a big payday, the right time or a significant event. When you have the opportunity, take it and use it. Deal with the consequences later. And if the opportunity doesn't present itself, have a

safety plan that will get you away. Do everything you can to stay alive and as soon as the moment presents itself, seize it.

The Healing Process Begins

After confronting the perpetrator and taking the necessary steps to leave the situation, you should begin the healing process immediately. It doesn't matter the magnitude and severity of the harm, manipulation or abuse you have suffered. You need to be able to move past it and waiting for time to "heal" your wounds requires more than simply sitting on the couch and reliving the past. Time will give you enough distance from your experience, but if you've learned anything from this book, it's that emotional scars almost never heal completely. If you don't do something about it, an unhealthy scab could form over the wound, leaving you just as vulnerable as before, if not more so. Talk to a counselor, go to therapy, whatever you choose to do, take an active role in facilitating the healing process. It won't happen overnight, but you can be sure that with each day and each step you take in therapy, you will be closer to getting better.

Don't Cover The Truth

"It's not the original scandal that gets people in more trouble ... it's the attempt to cover it up."
- Tom Petri.

Face the Truth

Going through something as difficult and traumatic as living with the lies of someone you trust can have a profound psychological effect. When I started this book, my goal was to help people filter out the lies in their everyday environment and live above the manipulations of others. The main focus of this book has largely been to help you look inward and understand what dark psychology really is. However, there is one aspect that we have not addressed: the people who perpetrate these acts.

The people who are most likely to use and manipulate you are those you have come to love and trust. The length of the relationship does not guarantee that they are incapable of hurting you. Sometimes, time spent together cements your trust in them, making you more vulnerable to their charms. Not everyone who enters your life will end up manipulating you, but neither do strangers pose less of a threat. There is no simple way to determine if a person is going to hurt you. The best you can do is to watch for the above signs and keep an open mind because you may have more difficulty with the idea that someone you trusted has hurt you than with the act itself.

Accepting the Painful Truth

In such a situation, your first impulse will be to deny. This denial will do you more harm than good. Instead of covering up the truth, you must face it head on. Recognize the situation for what it is. Don't let your emotions cloud your ability to make rational decisions. Because yes, being manipulated sucks and the people who do it deserve some sort of punishment, but we all know things are often more complicated than that. What if the person is your sister, brother, spouse, best friend, spiritual leader? How do you deal with it?

Start by accepting that their status in your life does not automatically make them immune to the consequences of their actions. But there are other factors that could be affected by any decision you make. So, first, face the embarrassing truth. Acknowledge that they have failed and hurt you with their deceptions and actions. Then, decide if the relationship is worth continuing. Did your partner cheat on you and lie to you all this time? That's terrible, but do you really want that to be the end of that relationship? Are there children involved? What happens if you suddenly cut your partner off? You need to know that in a situation like this, cutting the person off is not the only answer.

Making Rational Decisions

Ask yourself the right questions. What was the relationship like before the offense? Was it good? Is it worth saving? Is the person willing to put in the effort necessary to make things right? Are you willing to put in that effort?

If you decide to end the relationship, you need to think about how to handle the relationships that are linked to this breakup. If there are no ties, proceed to the next chapter on forgiving yourself. If there are ties, depending on their nature, you may both need to work out a narrative about how to proceed. If those ties are fragile, you can simply go your separate ways without giving anyone further information, as you owe no one any explanations. Do your best to heal and move on without damaging other relationships unless absolutely necessary.

If you decide to continue the relationship, both of you will have an arduous road ahead of you. It will be a difficult and long battle. You will make it, no doubt, but not without will and effort.

Rebuilding Trust

Both parties must show a willingness to heal the relationship. Apologizing profusely is a good start, but they must do more than that. The fabric of trust has been torn and repairing it will require time, effort and commitment. Both of you must be realistic in your expectations. The person who committed the fault will have to work hard to regain your trust, and the injured person will have to work hard to learn to believe in that person again. There will be failures initially, but what will keep things strong will be the renewed commitment to move forward day by day.

Recovery Process

To begin with, they may want to give themselves space after the initial crisis. This space can be anywhere from a few days to a couple of weeks, but should not exceed one month. Use this time to process your feelings about the incident. Try to separate the person from their actions, because, although their actions were hurtful, there are many factors that could have contributed to them. It may seem like you are making excuses, but you are not. Circumstances may lead people to take certain actions, but those actions do not completely define their character. If you have decided to repair this relationship, you may need to adopt this approach in your thinking.

Keep the line of communication open. I'm not saying you should analyze every thought, just don't shut each other out. Conversations may seem stilted at first, but over time, they will pick up the pace. Be honest in your conversations, but avoid speaking with resentment. Avoid bringing up the past in every discussion. Holding on to what has happened makes it difficult to move forward. Stay in the present. Remember, living in the past has no real benefit.

Confidence in your Decisions

Trust that you have made the right decision. When you discover that you have been manipulated and deceived, not only does your trust in others break down, but also in yourself. You question your judgment at every turn. Stay in the present and trust that you have made the right, rational decision to set things right. But don't put pressure on yourself by making it mandatory for the new relationship to work. Try hard, put in the time, but don't be disappointed if things don't work out the way you expected.

Forgiving Yourself

Finally, forgive yourself. We all make mistakes, and we can all be deceived. The important thing is to learn from the experience and move forward with more wisdom and strength.

Forgive Yourself

"Take a walk in the garden of forgiveness and pick a flower of forgiveness for all that you have done. When you come to the present moment, make a complete and total forgiveness of your whole life and smile at the bouquet in your hands, because it really is beautiful."
- Stephen Richards.

Self Forgiveness

People assume that when you have been wronged, the main party requiring forgiveness is the person who committed the offense. Usually, they are right. But in a situation like this, where a relationship was established with the offender and that offender took advantage of the relationship, one of the people who needs forgiveness is the victim. There is a reason why, even when ties have been severed with the offender, you still experience emotions such as depression, anger, irritability, anxiety and mood swings. These are normal emotions, but you may not be experiencing them for the reasons you think.

There is a strong possibility that the reason for all these emotions is guilt and shame. This guilt does not stem from something you think you did wrong. It is rooted in the thought that you did something you should not have done. You feel guilty for being gullible, vulnerable and for putting yourself in a situation where you were easily manipulated. You feel guilty for the pain you think you caused yourself. We have all been in this situation at one time or another. We feel guilty that our actions or inactions led to the pain of others, even if we were not directly involved in the perpetration of the act.

It's important to remember that it wasn't your fault

The first thing you need to do is to remind yourself that, regardless of what happened, it is not your fault. You may not be able to change this perception overnight, but over time, by constantly reminding yourself of this fact, you will begin to believe it. To further affirm this belief, you must also remind yourself that the lessons you have learned from this experience have put you in a better position to protect yourself against similar incidents in the future.

Accepting the Past

The next thing is to accept that the past is not something you can change. It has already happened, you have learned and you have moved on. There is no need to keep reliving the experiences you had. Dwelling on the "what ifs", "what could have been", "what could you have done" cannot change a single second of what has already happened. The best you can do is to pick up the lessons learned and mold them into the new principles by which to live. You have bravely accepted the reality of the situation despite the lies you were told. Now is the time to accept that this matter was concluded in the past and there it stays. You may be dealing with the aftermath of the crisis, but that doesn't mean it's still happening. Take each day as it comes and find more reasons to look forward instead of looking back.

Redoing the Past Mentally

If you feel so anxious about the past, you can take a day to mentally recreate it. Write down what you think you could have done to change things, knowing what you know now. And then move on. The purpose of this exercise is to give you a sense of control over what has happened. Take back your power and move on to the next thing.

Overcoming Regrets

Now that you've rewritten the past, it's time to turn to the next page and begin the next chapter of your life. Start by addressing your regrets. These have a way of increasing our negative feelings. Accept that you did the best you could under the circumstances and give yourself room to grow. Remember, yours was not a crime. You were simply unlucky enough to trust the wrong person. Assign blame to the right person. Using statements like "I always fall for the wrong person" or "I'm so gullible" is very limiting. Dig deep within yourself to discover exactly where those thoughts are coming from. Only when you have identified the underlying emotion will you be able to overcome these negative affirmations. And the longer you access these negative statements, the more acute your anxiety levels will become. This is because you may become somewhat paranoid about your relationships with people, seeing enemies where there are only friends and reading wrong meanings into every action.

Recovering Self-Love

Finally, there is the issue of love. We can be hard on others, but the person we are hardest on is ourselves. We find it easier to forgive the perpetrator than to forgive ourselves, and the cost of this behavior is self-destructive patterns that are evident in our other relationships. We sabotage those relationships before they even begin. Under the guise of preventing another manipulative relationship, we destroy new relationships. The real reason for this behavior is the loss of a sense of self-love. Deep down, you don't feel you deserve love, but because you'd rather hear that from yourself, you burn bridges. There are pills to help you cope with anxiety and depression, but there are no pills to help you get to that place where you fall completely in love with yourself. That will take work and, at the end of the day, it's worth it. There are no hard and fast rules on how to begin this journey of self-discovery. However, I think waking up each day with positive affirmations like "I love myself and I deserve to be loved" is a good start. It may seem corny at first, but in the long run it is very effective.

Let Go

When you have resolved your issues with the past, forgiven yourself and begun the process of learning to love yourself, it is time to let go. All that pain, all that negativity, all that anger... accept it for a moment and then let it go. All the steps mentioned in this chapter are important, but the healing process is only complete when you let go.

Forgiving yourself is the final and most crucial step in breaking cycles of manipulation and deception. In doing so, you regain power over your life and open the door to a more authentic and happier existence.

Trust Your Instinct

The Importance of Instinct

In one of the previous chapters, we briefly touched on this subject. I decided to devote an entire chapter to it because, when faced with the forces of dark psychology, your main defense is your instinct. While your brain interprets signals based on facts, logic, and sometimes experience, your heart works at the opposite extreme, filtering information through emotions. Your gut is the only thing that picks up vibrations that neither the heart nor the brain can detect. If you can train yourself to recognize your inner voice and react to it, you reduce your chances of being seduced by people trying to manipulate you.

Recognizing the Inner Voice

To begin with, recognizing this voice is difficult. And that's because, throughout our lives, we have allowed the voices of doubt, self-criticism and criticism from others to drown out our authentic voice. This voice or instinct is focused on your survival. So, trust that when it is activated, it detects things in your immediate environment that your neurons cannot yet process. Some people call it intuition and others refer to it as instinct; they are certainly the same thing, especially when it comes to relationships.

To begin to trust your instinct, you must accept that it won't always make logical sense. If you've ever been in the middle of something and suddenly experienced the sensation of being watched, you know what I mean. You don't have eyes in the back of your head, there's no one else in the room, but you feel a slight chill and a "sudden certainty" that you're being watched. That's exactly what I'm talking about.

Uncluttering the Mind

The first step in connecting with your instinct is to clear your mind of the voices you have let in. You can do this with meditation. Forget the "he said, she said." Focus on your center, on that voice that you know is you. Then pay attention to your thoughts. Don't dismiss those eclectic monologues in your head. Instead, go with the flow of thoughts.

Why do you think a certain way about a person? Why do you feel so deeply about someone you've only known for a few days? What is that nagging feeling you have about another person? By exploring your thoughts, you become more attuned to your intuition and understand when it is activated and how to react to it. If you are the type who prefers to make impulsive decisions, you may need to learn to take a step back to pause and think. This moment of pause gives you the opportunity to reflect and evaluate your decisions.

Trusting Yourself and Others

The next step is difficult and not many people will be able to follow it. Unfortunately, it is not a step you can skip or evade. This step involves trust. In order to trust your instinct, you must be open to the idea of trusting yourself and others. Your inability to trust others will only make you paranoid and, when you are paranoid, it is not your instinct that is activated, it is your fear. Fear has a tendency to turn anything into a threat. You have to let go of your fear, embrace trust and let that guide your new relationships. Without the mental blocks that fear puts in your mind, you will be better able to listen to the inner voice.

Reevaluate Priorities

Finally, you need to reevaluate your priorities. If money and material possessions are at the top of your mind, you may not be able to see beyond them. Every interaction you have with people will be interpreted as an attempt to take advantage of you and, if you think about this long enough, it will soon become your reality. You know that you attract what you think about. If you are constantly thinking about material wealth, you will only attract people who think the same way.

Analyze Relationships

Use this as a guide to view all your relationships; old, new and potential ones with this new perspective. Don't go into a relationship expecting to be cheated on. Whether it's a business relationship, a romantic relationship or even a simple friendship, be open when approaching them. This way, you can get the right response from your intuition about them. Also, don't think that your instinct will tell you to run in the opposite direction when you meet suspicious people. It will be a little nudge.

A Personal Example

I remember an experience during one of my trips. I got into a cab. There was nothing physically evident that I could point to as a trigger, but I suddenly felt a revulsion toward the driver. I was overwhelmed by a smell of sweat. I'm not very sensitive to body odors, but I have been in situations where I simply had to hold it in [elevator, anyone?] But in this case, I wanted to get out of his cab. As soon as we got to a well-lit spot, I asked to get out, even though it wasn't my stop. Just as I got out, a patrol car pulled up next to it. Apparently, they had been notified of his involvement in a robbery and kidnapping case. I don't know if he had the same plans for me. All I knew was that as soon as I got in, I couldn't get out fast enough. My instinct didn't tell me to run or that my driver was a kidnapper. It just made me feel that there was something wrong with being in that car. It's just that simple.

Conclusion

In the same way, your gut will speak to you using a language you understand. Whether it's chills, goose bumps or a sudden urge to vomit, you'll recognize that feeling when you experience it and, with practice, you'll learn to trust it.

Practice the Best Principles in your dealings with others.

"Well, better, optimal. Never stop. Until your good is better and your best is optimal."
- St. Jerome.

The Law of Sowing and Harvesting

Christians have a saying, "You reap what you sow." It is more than a biblical phrase; it encapsulates the natural order of things. Sure, we know that sometimes bad things happen to very good people and vice versa. But, never believe for a moment that people don't get what they deserve. Because they do.

Breaking the Cycle of Pain

When you've been treated badly in life, you naturally want to shut yourself off and close your heart to others. And if you have to deal with people, you want to always position yourself where you have the upper hand. The problem with this way of thinking is that, because of your experiences, you become a victim who has decided, at least on a subconscious level, to make other people into victims.

You may find temporary pleasure in treating others the same way you were treated, but the long-term damage can be devastating. You could even set off a series of events with a domino effect that could come back to you. Even when presented with the opportunity, don't take it. Instead, choose to end the cycle of pain with you. As someone who has been in that situation, I can tell you it's not easy.

My Own Experience

As a teenager, I was painfully shy. I had a hard time talking to people. Even when I was with people like my parents and siblings, with whom I had lived my whole life, I didn't completely come out of my shell. But that all changed when I met Debbie. She was my high school dream and I remember being painfully in love with her.

It took me a long time to work up the courage to ask her out. And when I did, I was even more surprised that she said yes. I was on cloud nine for the next three months until I found out it was just a bet. Yes, I know it sounds remarkably like that teen movie that was a hit back in the day, except this time, I was the victim. It hurt more than words can say and that wasn't the worst of it. I was humiliated in the worst way a person like me could be.

I'm not sure how I made it through that month at school, much less the school year, but I did. Moving forward to my post-college years, I ran into Debbie again. Let's just say I was in a more advantageous position and had the option of using my position to make life difficult for her, but I chose not to.

Initially, she interpreted this as me still having feelings for her and tried to use that to her advantage. I politely informed her that I was just doing my job. Had I maintained the feelings I had for her in the past, she would have reacted differently. Either she would have succeeded in her attempts to seduce me or I would have been seduced into using the powers my position offered me to "punish" her. But I did neither. And in that decision, I found true freedom.

Don't Be the Dispenser of Justice

Life has a funny way of working things out. Don't take yourself as the dispenser of justice. Instead, arm yourself with the lessons you've learned and use them to your advantage. As St. Jerome said in the introductory quote, be the best version of you...even when you're on trial.

Conclusion

I have heard people warn saying, "the heart of man is desperately wicked." I don't know who said it or where I heard it, but it is etched in my mind and I find it to be true. There are no devices or software applications that can be used to decipher another person's thoughts. The best you can do is understand your own thoughts and feelings and do your best to live by your principles and values. But just because you can't tell whether or not your new best friend is betraying you doesn't mean you should obsess over it.

Yes, the true intentions of a man's heart are hidden. However, man's ability to do good is just as great as to go in the other direction, and this is not the best thing. The best thing is that for every person who has hurt you in the past, there are a hundred more who want to do good for you. It may sound unbelievable, but this is the reality of the situation. This book was not written to scare you into your shell and make you avoid dealing with people. On the contrary, I wrote it to help you make better decisions in your relationships.

By understanding the tricks and tools that certain people employ in their dealings with others, you are better equipped to protect yourself from those vices. And if you have been hurt by people, this book is meant to help you in the healing process. Nothing in life is concluded. We may have reached the end of the book, but that doesn't mean your process is over. If you take the lessons I have shared with you to heart, you can open yourself to the wonderful insights that life has in store for you. The journey to gain a deeper understanding of yourself and discover yourself is, in itself, a very rewarding experience.

So close this book, but keep your heart and mind open. Some of life's clichés have a tremendous impact on our lives. Love intensely, smile more and, most importantly, let go. Life is too precious and wonderful to live it any other way. And always wake up remembering that you deserve the best that life has to offer. Thank you for joining me on this journey.

Final Words

As we come to the end of this journey through the less traveled paths of human psychology, it is essential to reflect on what we have discovered together. This book has not only been an exploration of the darker corners of our psyche, but also an invitation to face and understand those shadows that, though we often fear, are fundamental to our integrity and personal growth.

I hope that, by immersing yourself in the pages of "**Discovering Dark Psychology**," you have found not only understanding, but also the strength to accept and transform the darkness into a light that guides your path. May each story, each theory and each revelation have better equipped you to face your own abysses and those around you with courage, understanding and, above all, with renewed hope.

Remember that darkness does not exist only to be feared or rejected. It also shapes our character, tests our resilience and sharpens our empathy. By embracing our full complexity, we can begin to live with greater wholeness and purpose, appreciating light and shadow alike as essential parts of our being.

Do not let this be the end of your exploration. Let the seeds planted in this book blossom into an ongoing quest for self-knowledge and human understanding. May your journey through dark psychology be a beacon that illuminates not only your darkest moments, but also the paths of those around you.

With each day, with each challenge, I invite you to choose empathy over judgment, curiosity over condemnation, and hope over fear. Thus, together, we can build a world where the light of our understanding shines on all shadows, not to eliminate them, but to understand them and, ultimately, to find in them our common path to redemption and renewal.

Thank you for allowing me to accompany you on this profound and revealing journey. May what you learn here resonate in your days, in your dreams, and in the countless ways you choose to be and relate to the world. Until our paths cross again in the pursuit of knowledge, go forward with courage, with an open heart, and above all, with inexhaustible hope.

Final Epilogue

As we close the pages of this book, it is not the end, but a new beginning. **"Discovering Dark Psychology"** has been more than a series of chapters on the shadowy aspects of human behavior; it has been an invitation to confront and reconcile ourselves with the parts of ourselves that we often prefer to hide or ignore.

This journey has been as much about discovery as it has been about redemption. In exploring dark psychology, we have unraveled the threads that weave the complexity of our actions, our fears, and our hopes. I hope this book has served not only as a mirror to reflect our multifaceted nature, but also as a flashlight that illuminates a path to understanding and acceptance.

Bringing what you learn in these pages to everyday life is the true challenge and gift of this knowledge. Every interaction, every conflict, every moment of doubt becomes an opportunity to apply greater empathy, deeper analysis and more expansive compassion. With this new understanding, you can transform not only your own life, but also positively influence the lives of those around you.

The world needs people more than ever who not only understand the light and darkness of human nature, but who are committed to making understanding a bridge to acceptance and change. Your journey with this book could be the first step toward greater awareness of how our shadows can, if properly understood, direct us toward our brightest light.

With hope and courage, I invite you to carry forward the knowledge you have acquired, to share it generously and to allow it to illuminate not only your own paths, but also those in which you can guide others. May this book be not just a reading, but a transformation; not an ending, but an impulse towards new ways of living, understanding and loving.

Ultimately, **"Discovering Dark Psychology"** is a promise that understanding is the harbinger of change, and that each of us has the power not only to confront the darkness, but to redefine it and use it to forge a future filled with light and hope.

Thank you for joining us on this journey. May the seeds of understanding planted here blossom into a garden of wisdom and new perspectives in your life and in the lives of others. Until we meet again in the pages of another journey, keep walking with curiosity, courage and compassion.

ABOUT THE AUTHOR

Professional Background: YLICH TARAZONA is a renowned psychotherapist, writer and international speaker. He is also a Master Coach with NLP and Master Trainer in Neurolinguistic Programming. He specializes in alternative therapies, Ericksonian hypnosis, Emotional Freedom Technique (EFT - Tapping) and energy healing. He is considered one of the most prominent and influential professionals in the field of personal excellence by the various media.

He is destined to leave a legacy in the lives of millions of people through his passion, enthusiasm, dynamism and principled leadership. He is the creator of Hypno Reengineering and Mental Bio Reprogramming, two online systems dedicated to providing coaching in the consolidation of competencies and development of maximum human potential.

Its methodology is designed to enhance the competencies of the individual through a sequence of sessions and therapies, which aim to guide the coachees to find the necessary tools that will allow them to reach their goals, achieve their objectives and consolidate results in their areas of excellence.

He is the author of the Reingeniería y BioProgramación Mental series of books and conferences, including: "**Program your mind and determine your future**", "**Heal myself and free yourself from self-sabotage**", "**The power of change and personal reinvention**", "**Discover your purpose and find your destiny**", "**The power of goals and the achievement of objectives**" and "**Consolidate your personal brand**", among others.

He is also the creator of the book "**Hidden Enigmas of Hypnosis**" and the course "**Practical Hypnosis**". These works deal with ancient and modern hypnosis in a professional, clear and easy to understand way. His approach is focused on helping readers or participants understand what trance and hypnotic phenomena are, as well as sharing a wide variety of techniques, suggestions, inductions, suggestibility tests, covert tests, convincers and deepeners, therapeutic and linguistic elements used by the hypnotist or hypnotherapist to generate hypnotic states and provoke the necessary changes in the individual's subconscious mind.

In terms of his **PURPOSE**, **mission** and personal **vision**, YLICH TARAZONA aims to share with his readers the resources they need to move forward with determination, teaching them to clarify their ideas, set goals and develop action plans that will enable them to conquer their most cherished dreams, allowing them to create their own future, write the story of their own lives and forge their own destiny every step of the way.

His **MISSION** is to leave a mark that makes a difference in the lives of the people to whom he teaches and carries his message, transmitting a legacy that allows them to evolve in all the transcendental aspects of life, personally, spiritually, emotionally, professionally, academically and financially.

His **VISION** is to bring people hope and a therapeutic option that allows them to transform their lives and improve, helping them to develop that seed of greatness that everyone carries inside, motivating them to develop their full human potential, to the next level of success, generating an improved version of themselves and opening new opportunities that allow them to rediscover themselves on the road to personal transformation.

"I firmly believe that within each of us lies a seed of greatness and a vast reservoir of unlimited potential that usually lies dormant, waiting to be discovered and developed, to blossom into our outer world. When each of us awakens that individual potential, we will rediscover our mission and the purpose that gives meaning to our lives, in a new conscious awakening. This is what I call, Reinvention and Personal Reengineering" **YLICH TARAZONA.**

Other Publications, Special Editions and Books Created by the Author

Dear reader, it was a pleasure to have shared with you this time of reading, I hope you have enjoyed to the maximum the information contained in this book that with so much affection I have prepared for you. Your great friend YLICH TARAZONA.

If you liked the content of my books, and would like to know more about my other publications, here is a list of all my books.

Updated Book List (JULY 2024):

Most Outstanding Novels:

✓ **Chronicles of the Guardians**: In Search of the Sacred Relics.

✓ **Reflections of the Abyss**: *A Leap of Faith* - A Journey of Redemption through the Darkness.

✓ **The Way of the Samurai** - *The Birth of a Warrior.*

Non-fiction book.

1. **"Awaken Your Greatness**: How to Program Your Mind to Discover Your Authentic Self". *Learn how to Transform your Life and Awaken your Inner Power.*
2. **"Inner Healing**: Break Chains and Free Yourself from Inner Self Sabotage". *Learn to Strengthen Your Inner Warrior and Master Your Emotions and Thoughts.*
3. **"Reinvent Yourself**: The Magic of Personal Transformation". *Innovation and Empowerment of the Self to create an Improved Version of Yourself.*
4. **"Purpose and Destiny**: The Compass of your Existence". *Discover the Principles and Connections for Living a Purposeful Life.*
5. **"Make the Difference**: Position your Personal Brand at the Top". *Strategies to Stand Out in a Competitive World.*
6. **"Goals and Objectives**: The Art of Strategic Planning". *A Step-by-Step*

Guide to Consolidate Your Dreams and Achieve Success.

7. "**Mental Re-Engineering**: The Art of Redesigning your Thoughts". *Learn how to Reprogram your Mind for Success and Begin your Personal Reinvention Process.*

8. "**Habits of Excellence**: The Path to Wholeness". *Secrets for a Healthy, Full and Happy Life.*

9. "**Inner Harmony**: Secrets of Life Coaching for a Life of Wholeness and Balance." *From Self-Awareness to Success. A Step-by-Step Guide to Personal Growth.*

10. "**Transform Your Life with NLP**: A Practical Guide to Neurolinguistic Programming for Effective Personal Change." *Master Effective Techniques and Methodologies for Deep Personal Transformation.*

11. "**The Art of Persuasion**: Discover the Power of Figurative Language and Metaphors in Communication." *Become a Persuasive Communicator through the Power of Metaphors and Allegories.*

12. "**Applied Hypnosis**: A Practical Manual for Developing Hypnotic and Persuasive Skills." *Acquire the Skills to Hypnotize and Persuade Effectively and Ethically.*

13. "**Hypnotize Effectively**: A Practical Course for Mastering Hypnosis in Any Context." *Learn the Secrets to Hypnotize Anyone, Anytime, Anywhere.*

14. **Hypnosis to the Next Level**: "Hidden Enigmas of Hypnosis Unleash the Power of your Mind and Transform your Reality." *Discover the Secrets of Hypnosis to Transform your Life.*

15. "**Quantum Awakening**: Mental Reengineering and Bio-Programming for Personal Evolution and the New Age of Thought." *Make a Quantum Leap in your Personal Evolution and Open the Doors to the New Age of Thought.*

16. "**Neuro-Oratory and Hypnotic Persuasion**: Discover the Art of Influencing with the Power of your Words." *Develop Persuasive Communication Skills and Power your Influence in Everyday Conversations.*

17. "**Engrams and Neural Consciousness**: Exploring the Relationship between the Conscious and Subconscious Mind." *Deepens the*

Relationship between Consciousness and Perception.

18. **"The Power of the Subconscious Mind**: Take Control of your Thoughts and Program your Mind for Success." *Discover the Unlimited Potential of your Subconscious to Transform your Life.*

19. **"Mastery in Life Coaching with NLP**: Mastering Techniques and Methodologies for Goal Achievement." *Learn the Essential Coaching Tools to Guide Others to Success.*

20. **"Multilevel Network Marketing**: Discover Network Marketing Opportunities in the Digital Age" *Open your Path to Financial Freedom with Effective Network Marketing Strategies.*

Always keep in mind that: "Constant learning, continuous training and permanent study are the keys between those who achieve success and those who do not". **YLICH TARAZONA.**

You can contact me directly through my website:

https://ylichtarazona.com/

COPYRIGHTS

Don't miss out!

Visit the website below and you can sign up to receive emails whenever Ylich Tarazona publishes a new book. There's no charge and no obligation.

https://books2read.com/r/B-A-PAIU-AXSUD

Connecting independent readers to independent writers.

Did you love *Discovering Dark Psychology*? Then you should read *Unraveling Dark Psychology*[1] by Ylich Tarazona!

Unraveling the Dark Psychology"Reflections and Revelations on the Hidden Nature of the Self."Discover the Dark Side of the Human Mind! And dive into the mystery revealed in this book.Have you ever wondered what lies behind the darkest actions of the human being?InUnraveling Dark Psychology, the author takes you on a haunting journey into the heart of human evil, exploring how and why people cross the line into the unimaginable. This book reveals the hidden forces that shape disturbing behaviors and challenges our traditional perceptions of morality and ethics."Unraveling Dark Psychology takes you on a journey through the darkest recesses of the human mind. This eye-opening book challenges you to confront what lurks in the shadows, that which influences our deepest decisions and obscures our true desires."Unraveling Dark Psychology" is not just a book; it is a revelation of the deepest and darkest mysteries of human psychology. Each chapter invites you to explore the hidden

---

1. https://books2read.com/u/mg85a6

2. https://books2read.com/u/mg85a6

truths behind the actions and thoughts that govern our lives, often without our knowledge.

Explore the depths of manipulation and control.

Discover how darkness shapes personality and relationships.

Transform your understanding of yourself and others.

Why Read This Book?

Illuminate the Hidden Corners: Discover how and why people use manipulative techniques in everyday life, from personal interactions to the professional arena.

Understanding Unconscious Influence: Learn about the subconscious factors that affect our decisions and behaviors, providing a new perspective on how we interact with the world.

Tools for Self-Discovery: This book equips you with the knowledge necessary to identify and counteract the hidden forces in your own life, promoting deep and lasting personal growth.

Topics of Interest:"Unraveling Dark Psychology" addresses a variety of topics that are essential for anyone interested in human nature:

Manipulation and Control: How these tactics are used in personal relationships and in society.

The Power of the Unconscious: Exploring how our minds hide truths that can set us free or shackle us.

Psychological Resilience: Developing mental toughness in the face of psychologically destructive tactics.

Ethics and Morality: How understanding dark psychology can lead to more ethical and morally conscious living.

Purpose of the Book:This book seeks not only to educate but also to empower its readers, offering them the tools necessary to navigate a world where dark psychology plays a constant and often hidden role. By the end of the reading, you will be more informed, alert and prepared to apply these teachings in your daily life, improving both your personal and professional relationships.This book is a must for:

Professionals and students of psychology, criminology, and social sciences.

Readers interested in the study of human behavior and ethics.

Anyone seeking to better understand the complexities of human nature to foster healthier relationships and safer communities.

Dive into the pages of Unraveling Dark Psychology and prepare to change your perspective on what it really means to be human.

Read more at https://ylichtarazona.com.es/.

Also by Ylich Tarazona

Applied NLP, Influence, Persuasion, Suggestion and Hypnosis
Hidden Enigmas of Hypnosis

Chronicles of the Guardians: In Search of the Sacred Relics
Chronicles of the Guardians: In Search of the Sacred Relics

Chronicles of Truth - Light Among the Shadows
Reflections of the Abyss: A Leap of Faith

Crónicas de la Verdad - La Luz entre las Sombras
Reflejos del Abismo: Un Salto de Fe

CRÓNICAS DE LOS GUARDIANES: En Búsqueda de las Reliquias Sagradas
Crónicas de los Guardianes: En Búsqueda de las Reliquias Sagradas

¡Desbloquea tu Creatividad! Secretos de Autoayuda Revelados

Desbloquea Tu Genio Creativo

Desbloquea tu Poder Interior: Domina la Hipnosis, PNL, Life Coaching y Neuro Oratoria
Enigmas Ocultos de la Hipnosis

Maestría en Oratoria y Comunicación Persuasiva
El Poder de Persuadir con tus Palabras

Mastery in Public Speaking and Persuasive Communication
The Power of Persuading with Your Words

Mind Manipulation Trilogy: Exploring the Mysteries and Enigmas of Dark Psychology
Unraveling Dark Psychology
Discovering Dark Psychology

Principes de base du succès et lois préliminaires du succès
Reprogrammez votre esprit et déterminez votre destin

Principi di base per il successo e leggi preliminari del successo
Riprogramma la tua mente e determina il tuo destino

Reprogram Your Mind and Determine Your Destiny
The Power to Heal Yourself
Discover Your Life Purpose
The Power of Goals
How to Build Your Personal Brand

Reingeniería y Reprogramación Mental
Reinvención Personal. El Arte de Rediseñar tú Vida
El Poder de Sanarte a Ti Mismo
Descubre Tu Propósito de Vida
El Poder De Las Metas
Cómo Construir Tu Marca Personal
Reprograma Tu Mente y Determina Tu Destino

Serie el Camino del Guerrero
El Camino del Samurái: El Nacimiento de un Guerrero

The Warrior's Path Series
The Way of the Samurai: The Birth of a Warrior

Transformando Tu Mundo: Guías Terapéuticas para una Vida Plena y Exitosa
Fortaleciendo tu Autoestima

Trilogía Manipulación Mental: Explorando los misterios y enigmas de la Psicología Oscura
Descubriendo la Psicología Oscura

Unlock Your Unlimited Potential! Self-Help Secrets Revealed
Unlock Your Creative Genius

Standalone
Despierta Tus Capacidades Oníricas
Awaken Your Dreaming Capabilities
Hábitos de Excelencia Para Vivir Una Vida Saludable
Habits of Excellence for Living a Healthy Life
Despierta tu Potencial Interior
Unlock Your Inner Potential
Disciplina Total: Toma el Control de Tu Vida y Alcanza el Éxito

Watch for more at https://ylichtarazona.com.es/.

About the Author

YLICH TARAZONA es un reconocido psicoterapeuta, escritor y conferencista internacional. También es Máster Coach con PNL y Máster Trainer en Programación Neurolingüística. Especializado en terapias alternativas, hipnosis Ericksoniana, técnica de liberación emocional (EFT — Tapping) y sanación energética. Es considerado uno de los profesionales más destacados e influyentes dentro del campo de la excelencia personal por los distintos medios de comunicación.

Está destinado a ejercer un legado en la vida de millones de personas a través de su pasión, entusiasmo, dinamismo y liderazgo

Read more at https://ylichtarazona.com/.

About the Publisher

Hola, permíteme presentarme. Soy **Ylich Tarazona**, un psicólogo, hipnoterapeuta, conferencista internacional y escritor. Mi pasión por el desarrollo humano me ha llevado a crear obras significativas como la serie **«Principios Básicos para Triunfar y Leyes Preliminares del Éxito»** que se componen de 7 libros extraordinarios que están enfocados en el empoderamiento del ser.

Además de mis estudios como psicólogo, me especialicé como **Máster Coach con PNL** y **Trainer en Programación Neurolingüística**. También tuve la oportunidad de especializarme en terapias alternativas, como: **Hipnosis ericksoniana**, técnica de liberación emocional (EFT-Tapping) y **sanación energética**. Lo que me permite poder emplear una variedad de metodologías, haciendo más efectivas mis aportaciones.

Se me ha reconocido en varios medios de comunicación como una de las figuras más destacadas en el campo de la excelencia personal. Gracias a mi pasión, entusiasmo, dinamismo y liderazgo centrado en principios. **Valores que están orientados a generar un impacto duradero en la vida de innumerables personas.**

Así mismo, soy el creador de un innovador sistema de Reingeniería y Bioprogramación Mental ®, un salto cuántico para la evolución del ser y el despertar de la conciencia.

Mi sistema de **Reingeniería y Bioprogramación Mental** ® es una metodología diseñada para ayudar a las personas a consolidar habilidades esenciales y desarrollar el máximo de su potencial humano. Gracias a que empleamos estratégicamente una serie de herramientas de **life coaching** combinadas con técnicas avanzadas de **hipnosis ericksoniana y programación neurolingüística**. Permite a los participantes obtener los resultados deseados.

Nuestra metodología única está diseñada para fortalecer las habilidades individuales de cada persona a través de una serie de sesiones y terapias. **El objetivo de este proceso de acompañamiento es guiar a cada cliente individualmente a encontrar las herramientas necesarias para alcanzar sus metas, materializar sus objetivos y obtener resultados efectivos en sus áreas de excelencia.**